FLOURISH

FLOURISH

7 WAYS GRATITUDE
CAN TRANSFORM YOUR LIFE

JENNIFER GARMAN

NEW DEGREE PRESS

COPYRIGHT © 2020 JENNIFER GARMAN

FLOURISH

7 Ways Gratitude Can Transform Your Life

ISBN   978-1-64137-511-5   *Paperback*

         978-1-64137-512-2   *Kindle Ebook*

         978-1-64137-513-9   *Ebook*

CONTENTS

———

ACKNOWLEDGMENTS

First and foremost, I want to give unending thanks to God for the motivation, drive, direction, and ability to turn an engineer into an author and make this book a reality.

To my husband Kyle, thank you for always believing in me and being my biggest fan. If it weren't for you, I would never have had the courage to take the risks and chase my dreams. I'm grateful and love you beyond words.

To my children—Jordan, Caden, and Emery, I am so proud to be your mom and for your support and love through this whole crazy journey. May you have the confidence to go for what you want, the courage to get back up after you fall, and the strength to persevere. I love you more than you will ever know, for eternity.

Mom, Dad, Beth, John, and Mark—thank you, I love you all!

To Eric Koester and New Degree Press—I would have never guessed I could have gotten to this point, let alone so quickly, and it's because of your expertise and guidance. I am forever grateful.

Last but not least, I would like to express my heartfelt gratitude to those who supported and helped me along the way—without you, this book would not have been possible. Barbara Garman, Traci Grover, Stacy Keppler, Linda Weber, Stephanie Snow, Maura Klutz, Frank Tanner, Elizabeth Smouse, Barclay Garman, Janet Tamassia, Kim Kocuba, Dani Page, Ginger Walley, Jen Hale, Steve Lacey, Pat Wallenhorst, Joy Morel, Steve Chiodini, Julia Phillips, Mark Garman, Amy Schalk, Betsy Delisi, Trina Medley, Danette Cooper, Sophie Walker, Mike Wallenhorst, Amy Lynne Helwig, Nikki Speer, Michelle Spott, Kelly Moskal, Beth Young, Tosha Woodard, Amanda Mason, Penny Williams, Joe Matsko, Stephanie Oates, Julie Hines, Krista Woods, Mindy Moger, Brooke Barber, Sam Lucania, Lisa Bergman, Melanie Saffell, Kimberly Zupfer, Nikki Shafer, and so many others.

INTRODUCTION

THE ABYSS

"Mommy, what's wrong? Are you sick again?"

My oldest daughter was so sweet and caring, but my mind went to my youngest. She was only three at the time, but I was hit with the thought that she would never remember who I was before I got sick. My twins would probably not remember much either. Tears welled up, and my eyes glossed over. The relentless insomnia, anxiety, depression, and brain fog had devoured me internally, and I felt like a shell of who I once was. The worst part was that I appeared healthy, which meant that even if I did tell someone what I was going through, I wasn't taken seriously. So eventually, I stopped. This was my reality for seven years—countless doctors, tests, false hopes. Seven years I will never get back.

"Sweetie, I'm just having a rough day today."

I fibbed, hoping she would be comforted by the temporary illusion, but I think she knew. At the young age of five, my daughter had taken on more of a caregiver role than any child should have to, and it broke my heart. I went to yet another specialist that day after I somehow managed to get my kids off to school, hoping for answers. I got blunt candor instead.

"I can't help you."

I don't know if it was shock or acceptance, but what the doctor told me that day sank in. Yes, something was wrong, but no one could determine what. Every test imaginable had been run without answers. I could crawl further down the rabbit hole than I already had, but deep down, I knew it would be futile. These words stung, but I needed to hear them.

The following banter I don't recall, but then he said something that at the time felt like pity, and I remember being insulted. Looking back, how I wish I would have taken those words seriously.

"Your thoughts have the power to help heal you or make you sick—even more sick than you are now."

I wish I had paid attention to that statement when I first heard it. Instead, I dismissed it as fluff, something he said to me because he didn't have any other advice, because not saying anything felt too uncomfortable. That doctor who couldn't help me didn't realize how much his final words would eventually be the key I needed.

Years later, when I was studying to become a life coach, I came across the notion of gratitude. It became a recurring theme in my studies and a cornerstone to a balanced and happy life. I was intrigued and took on gratitude as a side study, along with an obsession about happiness.

Could our thoughts really be this powerful?

I JUST WANT TO BE HAPPY

Do we have the potential to be happy here and now? If so, how do we attain that happiness?

Happiness seems elusive to so many. Most people will say they want happiness in life, yet almost everyone succumbs to the realization that happiness is somewhere in the future. I will be happy when I get that promotion, make "x" amount, get married, have kids, and the list goes on and on.

One thing is certain—setbacks will arise. We will lose loved ones, life will derail, and undesirable things will happen. How do we counteract all those setbacks and get back on track?

An effective way to counteract the negativity and set yourself on a path to happiness is not looking back or rushing too far ahead but staying in the present.

Longing for the future can create a sense of anxiety while fixating on the past can contribute to depression. That's not to say it's unhealthy to do both at times but living in the present as much as possible is a key trait for happiness and contentment.

Through studying, research, prayer, and conversation with so many others in my position, I finally realized I already had the most effective tools to facilitate healing and recovery—more than any doctor or pill could provide. God's answer to my prayers.

My motivation in writing this book is to help as many people as I can reach who may be suffering in solitude or feeling like they've exhausted all options. I am so excited to share what I have learned and will go deeper into my journey in the coming chapters.

If you had the tools and mental wherewithal to realize when you weren't happy and shift your mind-set to happy as easily as snapping your fingers, how powerful would that be? In Chapter 1, I will describe how gratitude enters the equation and why it can be so powerful.

We will explore seven ways that gratitude can impact one's life in a positive way, including:

1. Raising self-worth
2. Improving mental health
3. Boosting physical health
4. Handling adversity
5. Connecting to others
6. Increasing happiness
7. Gaining abundance

You'll also learn exactly how I used the tools I found in the "how-to" portion of this book. Additionally, I've included small takeaways at the end of each chapter so you can begin cultivating gratitude right away.

Our self-worth can be directly tied to how much gratitude we have in our lives, and the more we embrace gratitude, the better we feel about ourselves and our circumstances as outlined in Chapter 2.

In Chapter 3, we will explore the daunting subject of mental health. Are you or your loved ones affected by stress, anxiety, depression, or all the above? Gratitude can have a profound effect on one's mental health, and we will dig deep into the why.

Chapter 4 examines our physical health and how our bodies are tied to our mental state of being at the cellular and genetic level. One of the stories I share is an amazing miracle of this extraordinary connection between body and mind.

We can use a mind-set of gratitude to prepare for when bad things do happen—and it's not a question of if, but when. Chapter 5 tackles the ability to handle adversity and how our roots in gratitude can strengthen us for the countless disappointments, tragedies, and losses that happen over a lifetime.

We were made as energetic beings, all connected to each other. To pursue self-sufficiency, many of us have adopted the mentality that we don't need others, but we have an innate need for connection from the day we are born to the day we die. Cultivating gratitude can connect us to others, and we discuss this further in Chapter 6.

Chapter 7 examines the connection between gratitude and happiness. It's one of my favorite topics, and we will see how they are directly correlated.

Happiness, although exciting, is not even the best reward of gratitude. The overflowing abundance that comes from embracing gratitude is what we study in Chapter 8. A truly miraculous transformation has happened in my life since finding gratitude.

Most importantly, Scripture is tied in throughout this journey. What has been recorded in the Bible centuries ago is now converging with what's being discovered by science. Every discovery is proving the Bible to be true over and over again. I find it fascinating that the answers have all been there, yet our awareness of the truth is just coming into focus. Isn't it amazing that science is validating all the things said by Paul said in his letters to the Corinthians, Colossians, Thessalonians, Romans, Galatians, and Philippians true?!

The people in this book use gratitude as a powerful mind-set tool in their inspiring journeys and live happy fulfilling lives because of it. One such person I had the pleasure of speaking with, Matthew Maher, was a professional soccer player who seemingly had it all. When one poor decision lost him everything, he found gratitude, and his life's purpose grew beyond what he ever thought possible.

Maher's story is featured along with many others—including Tony Robbins, who has a ten-minute morning routine rooted in gratitude; Oprah Winfrey, who came from the humblest of beginnings and continually cites gratitude as her foundation; and Sheryl Sandberg, who lost her husband unexpectedly but found hope and resilience through gratitude. I've spoken to CEOs, addicts, and average people who have overcome insurmountable circumstances to find happiness and contentment in their lives through the chaos.

The chapters ahead also delve into numerous studies and research on the practice of gratitude and the many ways it can transform one's life for the better. We'll go on a fascinating journey into our raw scope of comparison and fixation on the negative. Why are kids always looking for things to be fair? Are we, in essence, doing the same? Once we understand our mind's comparison tendencies, we can choose to change our mind-set through gratitude.

We will dive deep into the ways to enrich your life as it is right now through the lens of gratitude and why this technique is so effective. This book explores the life-altering effects of gratitude in its many facets.

Everything I'm sharing in this book has been at the forefront of my thoughts for far too long. The mental health crisis our country is facing is at a critical point. We can't open a magazine without seeing another celebrity at the peak of success who took his or her own life. Mass shootings and gun violence are common daily news. Suicide has increased thirty-three percent from 1999 to 2017(age adjusted). In 2008, suicide ranked as the tenth leading cause of death for all ages in the United States, but in 2016, it had climbed to the second leading cause of death for ages ten to thirty-four, and the fourth leading cause for ages thirty-five to fifty-four.[1] Our youth are most at risk, and things need to change ASAP.

---

1   Centers for Disease Control and Prevention. "Suicide Mortality in the United States 1999-2017."

Social media is used by so many, but is it a double-edged sword? Can you think of times you "liked" a post but felt jealous, depressed, or some other negative emotion? The creators of Facebook admitted to exploiting our addictive tendencies and using dopamine conditioning to build market share. Beyond that, they conducted social experiments that were meant to negatively or positively affect a user's mood without their knowledge.[2] Many were outraged, but despite the breach of privacy, the user bases for platforms like Facebook continue to climb. In Chapter 3 we will explore in more detail why social media can be detrimental to our mental health, especially for children.

But where to start?

This book shares the research, science, stories, and methods to transform a life that is lacking to a life of true contentment, joy, and happiness. From all the research and implementation I have done in my own life over the past several years, I truly believe that gratitude is the catalyst to living in happiness every day. Neuroplasticity—or the ability for the brain to create new neural pathways and, in effect, change—helps us supercharge gratitude into a happiness juggernaut. Gratitude is not only the way to a fulfilling life, but a path to flourish, and you are about to find out why.

With gratitude,
Jennifer

---

2   Mike Allen. "Sean Parker Unloads on Facebook: 'God Only Knows What It's Doing to Our Children's Brains.'"

GETTING THE MOST OUT OF THIS BOOK

This book offers many ideas, but not all chapters may be applicable for your life and what you are hoping to learn. Each chapter contains stories, data, and suggestions that pertain to that topic.

FIRST AND FOREMOST

Gratitude is amazing and can absolutely transform your life, but one roadblock can derail the process. Before you can reap the full benefits of gratitude, you may need to address forgiveness. For many people, the lack of forgiveness holds them back, and the first step is forgiving ourselves.

"To forgive is to set a prisoner free and discover that the prisoner was you."

—LEWIS B. SMEDES

A fantastic resource is the ancient art of Ho'oponopono[3]. A Hawaiian practice of reconciliation and forgiveness. You can Google and find some great video resources to walk you through if you need to address forgiveness before moving on to gratitude.

DECIDE WHAT YOU WANT TO GET OUT OF THIS BOOK

What is missing or lacking that you most identify with? Each chapter's title is designed to help you, the reader, easily decide what speaks most to you. Additionally, at the end of each chapter is a small exercise. Practice these to start making an impact in your life right away. Use the numbered spaces to write down three areas in your life you want to improve, and then go find the answers.

1. _____

2. _____

3. _____

USE THE STRUCTURE ONLY AS A GUIDE

Keep in mind that although each chapter offers a stepping-stone to take action, the main implementation strategy is in Chapter 9. You may choose to read this book straight through, but you won't lose anything by skipping around, so feel free to read in the order your attention is grabbed. The most important part of this whole book is the implementation. You will want to dedicate ten to thirty minutes each day to practice what you have learned. We all have busy

---

3   "The Hawaiian Secret of Forgiveness."

lives, but as Tony Robbins once said, "If you don't have ten minutes, you don't have a life."

DON'T WORRY ABOUT MISSING OUT

If a chapter doesn't resonate with you, skip it. It's more important to concentrate on the areas that speak to you and then take consecutive action than to read the book cover to cover and implement nothing. Although gratitude has been scientifically proven to improve all seven areas in your life, it doesn't mean you are lacking in all of those areas. You can use this book as a happiness guide and refer to it as needed.

GET STARTED!

"A journey of a thousand miles begins with a single step."
— CONFUCIUS

Just jump in and get started! I guarantee if you take what's included in the action steps and dedicate ten to thirty minutes a day, you will see dramatic improvement in your life. Reading and implementing one to three chapters and taking the time each day to dedicate to the practices will help you gain momentum and encouragement to transform your entire life.

"Knowledge is not power; implementation is power."
— GARRISON WYNN

CHAPTER 1

IS HAPPINESS
REALLY A CHOICE?

"Happiness depends upon ourselves."

—ARISTOTLE

MY STORY

Nine years ago, my health fell off a cliff. It happened literally overnight.

At that time, my twins were three, and we had just celebrated my youngest daughter's first birthday. Life was chaotic but fulfilling. Each night, I would be woken time after time for this or that but fall right back to sleep, somehow getting a full night's rest—then I'd do it all over again without skipping a beat. I felt energetic during the day and rested enough when I woke, until one night I just couldn't fall asleep.

It wasn't due to anything in particular, and as I lay there, I remember thinking about how odd it was that I was so peaceful, yet I just couldn't doze off! Annoying as it was, I functioned the best I could the next day, knowing I would get a great night's sleep the following evening. But that night, the same thing happened, and the next night, and the next. Survival mode fully kicked in, and I was a mess by the time I got to the doctor. He chalked everything up to the stress of raising three young kids and sent me home with a sleep prescription.

Never being one to turn to medication, I remember how uneasy I felt taking the pills to cover up an unknown, underlying problem that was brushed under the rug. It took several nights, but the medication finally began working, and I got a bit of sleep. I wasn't able to get to sleep again without some sort of support for over seven years. And even though I was sleeping, it wasn't restful enough.

It wasn't just my sleep though—my health as a whole deteriorated along with it. Allergies developed out of nowhere to foods and environmental factors. I went from doctor to doctor who ordered test after test. When all the testing came back without answers, I made lifestyle changes based on a hunch here or there. Everyone seemed most concerned about the symptoms and treated those individually, which infuriated me more and more each day.

"You have Lyme."

"You have this or that autoimmune disease."

"You have x, y, and z."

Nothing I did helped much at all, and I succumbed to the fact that this might be my new reality, never getting back to the health I once took for granted. The worst part by far was that my kids didn't really know who their mom was. I functioned on a daily basis as best I could, often getting sick from everything and anything going around and being bedridden even more. I experienced a cyclical downward spiral.

I cried, prayed, and talked to anyone who would listen. Many people saw my outside appearance and didn't take me seriously. To be honest, I found that the hardest thing. Family connections and friendships changed. Occasionally I would come across another person who shared a similar plight, and

I would feel understood, but it was short-lived, as we each had to get on with life and didn't have extra time to wallow. I mostly tried to forget about how bad things were and pressed on. Sometimes, blips of time, I would get back to about seventy percent, and I lived those times to the fullest, enjoying my family and trips away, feeling so grateful. I hoped and prayed things would get back to the way they were before but lived in constant fear they would deteriorate further. Throughout my ordeal, I diligently kept researching and reading up on new things to try.

During one of my higher functioning periods, I decided to get my life coaching certification. The subject of happiness and its tie to gratitude came to the forefront while I studied. As mentioned in the introduction, I became obsessed with happiness, as I thought this was my new health reality. I needed to make the most of it, and heck, I had it so good compared to so many others and so much to be thankful for!

Happiness is so elusive for so many, I concluded, mostly because they were looking back at the past or envisioning future happiness. I was in this boat as well, thinking all too often that I would be happy when I got my health back, but the days and years passed by at an alarming rate while I waited.

I stumbled upon the million-dollar question: is happiness a choice? Yes and no.

A select few people out there can decide to be happy, and they are, but ninety-nine percent of us need more. We do need to decide we want to be happy, but that alone isn't enough, and we need to take action to get to that state of joy. Anyone can be happy, right now, if they decide they want to put in the work. And this is where gratitude comes in.

WHY GRATITUDE?

First, gratitude helps magnify your positive emotions so you're more likely to adapt to the good things happening in your life. Additionally, gratitude helps you counteract negative emotions like resentment, regret, and envy. Much research asserts that if you're grateful, you can't resent someone for having something that you don't. We will get into the data in the pages to come. The Webster definition of gratitude is an emotion of the heart, excited by a favor or benefit received; a sentiment of kindness or goodwill toward a benefactor; thankfulness.[4]

According to the UCLA Mindfulness Awareness Research Center, "regularly expressing gratitude (the quality of being thankful and the readiness to show appreciation) literally changes the molecular structure of the brain, keeps the gray matter functioning, and makes us healthier and happier."[5] Countless other studies exist on gratitude's benefits, and many will be explored in the coming chapters. For example, Tibetan monks' brains were scanned when they meditated and practiced gratitude, and their prefrontal cortexes lit up

---

4   Lynn M. Barton, Joan E. Sassone, and Mary Hasek Grenier. "Gratitude." In Webster.

5   Carrie D. Clark. "How Gratitude Actually Changes Your Brain and Is Good for Business."

like Christmas trees. The extent and immediacy of this reaction amazed the researchers.[6]

The Greater Good Science Center at UC Berkeley conducted a gratitude study with three hundred adults who were seeking mental health counseling at a university. The majority of these adults were grappling with anxiety and depression. The group that was asked to practice gratitude reported a significant increase in their mental health after the experiment concluded.[7] Other surprising benefits transpired during this study that we will explore more deeply in Chapter 3.

THE SURPRISING REALITY OF JUST HOW MUCH IT'S "IN YOUR HEAD"

My studies of happiness would always encompass gratitude and tie it so strongly together that it could not be ignored. Every study would either allude to or conclude that grateful people are happier people, so I began to practice and incorporate gratitude into my own life.

Around this same time, I happened upon the study of neuroplasticity. As I mentioned in the introduction, neuroplasticity is the ability of the brain to change and heal, especially in response to learning or experience or following injury.[8] I was fascinated and absorbed all I could from the work of Norman Doidge (psychiatrist, author and psychoanalyst), Annie Hopper (creator of the *Dynamic Neural Retraining System*), Caroline Leaf (neuroscientist and author), and Joe Dispenza

---

6   TodaSyo. "Matthieu Ricard's Approach to Meditation (Mystical Brain)."

7   Robert Emmons. "Why Gratitude Is Good."

8   Barton, Lynn M., et al. "Neuroplasticity." *In Webster*.

(neuroscientist and author). Story after story revealed people who overcame devastating injuries, hopeless diagnoses, and healed with neuroplasticity.

Shortly into my research, I came across a study about lottery winners, paraplegics, and baseline happiness. I was awestruck by the fact that after about six months, when the shock wore off, both lottery winners and paraplegics returned to the baseline happiness that they had been at before their life-changing event occurred. What an eye-opening fact! Our circumstances don't dictate our happiness—it's our choice.[9]

The power of the mind is amazing if we focus on all we do have—the key is staying positive and keeping that focus. This is where gratitude comes in. The rest of this book is an in-depth exploration of several key ways gratitude can be transformative.

SCIENCE AND SCRIPTURE CONVERGE

Our minds are more powerful than anyone previously imagined, and it's becoming more evident with the neurologic research being done. The thought patterns we choose are literally creating our reality. Dr. Caroline Leaf, a renowned neuroscientist and author of *Switch on Your Brain*, has done extensive research on the connection between our thoughts and our level of happiness.

Additionally, she has tied in Scripture throughout her book to back up her scientific findings. It's fascinating to see how

---

9   Philip Brickman, et al. "Lottery Winners and Accident Victims: Is Happiness Relative?" (917)

science is confirming Scripture, not contradicting it. Many passages in the Bible speak about the power of our mind and thoughts. Once thought to be Christian naivete, these truths are now being proven by science, as Dr. Leaf's book compounds on. Our minds are powerful, and our thoughts shape who we are and will become.

Today I have given you the choice between life and death, between blessings and curses. Now I call on heaven and earth to witness the choice you make. Oh, that you would choose life, so that you and your descendants might live!

DEUTERONOMY 30:19 NLV

THE SKY'S THE LIMIT

I had the power to transform my life. The incorporation of gratitude altered my life for the better, but when I tied it to neuroplasticity techniques, my transformation really took off. Scientific research is just starting to scratch the surface of understanding how complex and powerful an organ the brain is, but my practice of gratitude, in just a few weeks, was healing me more than anything else I had tried. The health I was enjoying was magnified by the grateful life I was living, and I was happier than I had been in years.

In the last few years, with my newfound health, I started my own company, took a product I designed from concept to market, appeared in numerous publications and on national TV, and wrote this book. To say I was on fire is an understatement; I have more energy and better health than ever before, and I knew I needed to share what I had learned with others. What I have for you is not some magic formula. It's not New

Age or transcendentalist. It is scripturally and scientifically based, and it takes work. However, I can tell you from first-hand experience that it's transformational. Are you ready?

CHAPTER 2

SELF-WORTH

——

"If you want to turn your life around, try thankfulness. It will change your life mightily."

—GERALD GOOD

STARTING FROM THE BOTTOM

Sam admittedly had everything any child could need. He grew up in a loving, religious, middle-class family in affluent northern Virginia. He remembers nothing negative in his early years. However, he kept having bouts of anxiety for seemingly no reason. He remembers being twelve and accosted by this out-of-control emotion that he hated but couldn't manage. He felt helpless with no resources to counteract the awful sensation. That feeling of anxiety followed him around everywhere; he couldn't shake it or escape it.

"The feeling was overpowering and relentless—at school, at home, at night in my head," Sam said.

When he was in middle school, he wasn't smart, popular, or athletic, and he didn't feel like he fit in or had a place. Worse, he felt like he stood out to others—he envisioned what they saw when they looked at him, and it wasn't good in any way. Sam thought perpetually of how others viewed him, and he cared about what they thought more than anything.

"I was comparing my insides to other people's outsides."

His self-worth took a huge hit because of where he went in his mind through others' eyes. He dreaded waking up and going to school because he had to relive his mental nightmares when he walked the halls, knowing he didn't fit in and fearing the disdain of others he'd created in his own mind.

"The only thing I knew for sure was that I hated the feeling and would do anything to escape it."

Eventually, he found a few kids who were willing to accept him because he would do "stupid stuff." He became the kid who would drink what was in the cup, take that pill, do that dare. He describes it as a slippery slope because he made the connection that when he partook of the drugs, it took the anxiety away. He then felt relieved for that moment, and it was therapeutic—his escape. Substances made the pain go away, and he lived in the new self-worth that the drunkenness or high would afford. He fit in, felt like himself, and was free. To a point. He soon found himself an addict, not even knowing what he'd done.

Sam knew no limits to his escapism and became sly in how he would get his next high. He convinced doctors to write him prescriptions and found pills from medicine cabinets and drawers in people's homes. This led him deeper and deeper into the black abyss of desperate survival, waiting only for the next high to escape from reality, no matter the risks to his life.

He describes going into friends' and families' homes and knowing exactly where to look for prescription medications. No one even attempted to hide them.

"It's akin to leaving a loaded gun in the same place in your home for children, visitors, or anyone who could be tempted to try," he tells me. That's a powerful, terrifying statement, but Sam shares a message of hope for those whose lives may be spiraling.

"The first step you need to get out of a hole is to stop digging," he says. But with addiction, he couldn't ease out of it, so he found himself in direr circumstances—eventually leading to multiple arrests and time behind bars.

Then fate intervened, and he met a girl named Rachel. She wasn't another addict or someone who had self-esteem issues, and she was interested in Sam for who he was, flaws and all. Rachel was someone worth changing his life for. She reintroduced him to the church, and life was seemingly perfect for a short time. He thought he had it under control. For a while, he could shake the unwanted desires and addiction.

Sam tells the story of a drowning man who is out at sea and praying to be saved. A boat comes by and offers him a life preserver, which he refuses, stating, "I'm praying and God will save me." Then a helicopter comes by and offers to drop a basket, but again he states that God will save him. Still praying, he sees a dolphin come up to him but doesn't grab on. He then drowns.

"Why didn't you answer my prayer?" he asks God.

God replies, "I sent you a boat, a helicopter, and a dolphin, and you refused to be helped."

"Jesus looked at them and said, 'With man this is impossible, but not with God; all things are possible with God.'"

MARK 10:27 NIV

Even though things were good in Sam's life for the first time he could remember, an addict is only as strong as his willpower, or lack thereof. He doesn't remember the night of his relapse. His only recollection was waking up in the hospital, gagging on the ventilator tube in his throat—his life preserver. It was a searing, painful shock back into consciousness, but it was not from a dream. In a haze of life-saving drugs and scorching pain, he had one captivating emotion.

Gratitude.

At that moment, he thanked God that he was alive. He was shown his medical chart and was told over and over that he shouldn't have awoken, he should have had severe brain damage, and his recovery was a miracle.

That was the moment he knew he wasn't strong enough on his own to beat his addiction. He needed help from others.

Sam outlines what he calls his "holy trinity of recovery": physical, mental, and spiritual fitness. He built a network of help around him. He turned to these people in moments of weakness and prayed with them for strength each day. He is now sober, and he and Rachel recently welcomed their second son. Sam lives a life of gratitude daily, and he goes around to as many schools as he can and shares his story of addiction and hope. At the end of each talk, he offers anonymous help to anyone who is struggling with feelings of anxiety, depression, addiction, inadequacy, weakness, or low self-esteem, and he personally responds to each of them. He meets kids in person, if requested or needed, and is truly invested in helping as many as he can.

"It's not like it ever ends, though," Sam says. "I still go to meetings and still lean on my sponsor. It's like that with my trinity—without three legs to my chair, I'm going to fall down."

"But the LORD said to Samuel, 'Do not consider his appearance or his height...The LORD does not look at the things people look at. People look at the outward appearance, but the LORD looks at the heart.'"

1 SAMUEL 16:7 NIV

Sam's story is a wonderful example of redemption, the power of gratitude, and its tie to hope and self-worth. He found in gratitude a career of helping others, sharing how one seemingly scary word is the first place to start—help. What I love about Sam's story is that in the lowest point of his life, he felt the glorious hope and joy that gratitude brings. It moves me to tears how he must have felt waking in that hospital bed with a tube down his throat and choking, yet so grateful for life.

Interestingly, a study was published about the link between patients recovering from addiction and spirituality. As Sam concluded, almost all of the participants also cited a need for voluntary spiritual belief to get them through their addiction.[10] Addiction is so powerful that once entrapped, it's virtually impossible to beat alone.

We are all connected—energetically speaking—and we need to tap into that connection to pull out of the severe isolation that addiction causes. The study also addresses that a lack of spirituality manifests as bitterness rather than atheism. The hope was always there—it just needed to be realized. Our connection to others is important, but the connection to God is infinitely stronger, and with that comes not only hope but also a direct tie-in to happiness.

Sam's story oozes with the transformative power of gratitude. That he would wake on the brink of death, after experiencing a living hell, and feel overwhelming gratitude to be alive—to have a beating heart, be able to breathe, and take in his surroundings—that's amazing. Much of gratitude is recognizing what could have—or in Sam's case, what should have—happened. He was truly given a second lease on life, another chance that so many do not get, and he felt it so deeply that day in the hospital that his life changed for the better.

All of his experiences of addiction and the lowest lows of anxiety and depression came full circle through Sam's near-death experience. He awoke to fully live in the moment, immersed in gratitude and a vital sense of purpose and self-worth. Sam was the caterpillar who entered the cocoon and was transformed into a butterfly.

---

10   Adrienne Heinz, et al. "A Focus-Group Study on Spirituality and Sub-stance-User Treatment." (134)

VULNERABILITY AND SELF-DOUBT

"The inner speech, your thoughts, can cause you to be rich or poor, loved or unloved, happy or unhappy, attractive or unattractive, powerful or weak."

—RALPH CHARELL

Self-doubt can creep into anyone's life, even those who research and study the human psyche for a living.

As a researcher, Dr. Brené Brown has spent her career studying courage, vulnerability, shame, and empathy. Twelve years of her life were dedicated to researching vulnerability alone. She is world-renowned for her own vulnerability, giving everyone a window into her life's imperfections. An author of five self-help books, a social media contributor with over 1.5 million daily followers, and an advisor to Oprah are just a few of her accolades.

She opens up that she made the mistake of reading the comments in a newsfeed in a 2013 interview for Oprah's Super Soul Sunday show.[11] She goes on to describe human cruelty at its lowest as people hiding behind their anonymous posts, lashing out with cutting words such as "less research, more Botox," "drop at least twenty pounds," and worse.[12]

Brown admits to getting caught up in the whirlwind of social media comments and feeling deeply hurt, until she happened

---

11   Dr. Brené Brown. "Joy: It's Terrifying."
12   Dr. Brené Brown. "Shame Is Lethal."

upon a quote from Theodore Roosevelt that turned things around for her:

It is not the critic who counts; not the man who points out how the strong man stumbles, or where the doer of deeds could have done them better. The credit belongs to the man who is actually in the arena, whose face is marred by dust and sweat and blood; who strives valiantly; who errs and comes short again and again, because there is no effort without error and shortcoming; but who does actually strive to do the deeds; who knows the great enthusiasms, the great devotions; who spends himself in a worthy cause; who at the best knows in the end the triumph of high achievement, and who at the worst, if he fails, at least fails while daring greatly, so that his place shall never be with those cold and timid souls who know neither victory nor defeat.[13]

How easy is it to sit back and judge others for their flaws? How often do we do it without thinking twice, whether we voice it or not?

Failures are never discussed or acknowledged, yet without them, we would have no great victories or growth. Sadly, our society wants to sweep them under the rug when they should be celebrated as much as any achievement, for they are inevitable and necessary.

Those who live life rather than stand on the sidelines experience all that life has to offer. Looking back, those times I

---

13   Theodore Roosevelt. *Theodore Roosevelt's The Man in the Arena Speech: 100th Anniversary.*

persevered despite great fear were the times I grew the most, regardless of the outcome.

A light bulb turned on for Brown, and she realized she was in the arena, putting herself out there and getting dirty, not hiding behind a curtain trying to cut someone down to make themselves feel better. The thought then struck her, "If you are not in the arena getting your butt kicked on occasion, I'm not interested in your feedback." She challenges anyone to say something to her face, in front of her children even, and then duck!

People need to be more open about their shortcomings and failures. When we own our failures, real leadership can happen. We need to embrace our imperfections, work to overcome them, take risks, and be brave enough to share them. Most importantly, Brown states, we need to "challenge the false stories we make up when we experience disappointment." Her willingness to share her own struggles is what makes her so wildly popular and relatable, and why her *TED Talk* on vulnerability is one of the top five viewed videos of all time—with 45 million views and counting.[14] Her words resonate deeply: "Vulnerability sounds like truth and feels like courage."

I find such power and conviction in vulnerability. We all have shortcomings and fail on occasion, but it takes such strength to get back up, dust off, and try again with the knowledge of what didn't work before. Our society shuns failure, yet everyone who has reached success has admitted to failure again and again. In many cases, those with the most failures have

14   Brené Brown. "The Power of Vulnerability."

reached the highest success. "Only when we are brave enough to explore the darkness will we discover the infinite power of our light," Brown says. How different would things be if we embraced the ugly, celebrated the falls, and showed our kids that the true path to success isn't a steady upward climb to the top, but many downs mixed in. According to Brown, the uncertainty and risk of vulnerability is the "birthplace of love, belonging, joy, courage, empathy, and creativity."

"Each time we face our fear, we gain strength, courage, and confidence in the doing."

—THEODORE ROOSEVELT

VULNERABILITY TO GRATITUDE

But wait, this book is about gratitude, so why this divergence into vulnerability and shortcomings? "The relationship between joy and gratitude was one of the most important things I found in my research," Brown says. "I wasn't expecting it. In my twelve years of research on eleven thousand pieces of data, I did not interview one person who had described themselves as joyful who also did not actively practice gratitude." It seemed counterintuitive to Brown, and she admits going into her research thinking that if you were joyful you would be grateful, not the other way around. Instead, she discovered that "practicing gratitude invites joy into our lives."

Brown says this was so impactful that it changed her own life and the way she and her family live every day. After her family says grace before dinner, everyone shares something that they are thankful for. At first, her kids scoffed, claiming that she was experimenting on them for her research. But now they won't let the gratitude tradition of dinner be overlooked. Even on busy nights when everyone seems rushed, they remind the family to state something they are grateful for before eating.

"It's been extraordinary because not only does it invite more joy into our house, it also is such a soulful window into what is going on in my kids' lives." Some days, Brown's children are thankful for sitting far away from a sibling, but other days, they are grateful for their mom's health after seeing a friend experience the loss of her mother.

"Not only did it make us all more aware of what we had and more willing to slow down and really be thankful for the joyful moments we had, but it also let me know where she was emotionally in her life." She ends quoting a Jesuit priest, David Steindl-Rast, who said, "It's not the joy that makes us grateful, it's gratitude that makes us joyful."[15]

I couldn't agree more with Brown's realizations. In my own life, studies, and observations, the more gratitude you express, the happier you are. That's not to say we don't have bad days, aren't set off by others or circumstances, or don't get into ruts, but the stronger our gratitude muscle is, the quicker we can shift our minds back to plenitude.

---

15 Brené Brown. "Joy and Gratitude."

"She is clothed with strength and dignity, and she laughs with-out fear of the future."

PROVERBS 31:25 NLT

PUTTING IT INTO PRACTICE

Everyone needs to start somewhere, and sometimes you have nowhere to go but up. At those times, you can be grateful for something as simple as your breath. Contemplate the miracle of your existence and any function of the body, and I dare you to not feel in awe and grateful. This can be a simple five-minute breathing exercise, best done upon waking and before bed. Focus on your breath and start by counting to five slowly as you inhale and back down from five at the same pace as you exhale, pausing between breaths. Now, as you take in air, feel every cell in your body receive the oxygen it needs to flourish. In turn, every process in our body continues to function and we live. What a miracle it is that we are alive. If we take just a few minutes to contemplate this, it's difficult not to be in awe, and we can feel gratitude for that. Embrace this feeling of gratitude. Try to keep that feeling for as long as you can. This is how it begins. It may seem difficult at first, but like anything learned, it gets easier the more you do it.

We will explore more ways to incorporate and practice gratitude at the end of each chapter and focus on it as a whole in Chapter 9.

CHAPTER 3

MENTAL HEALTH

———

"It is impossible to feel sad or have any negative feeling when you're grateful. If you are in the midst of a difficult situation, look for something to be grateful for."

—RHONDA BYRNE

To establish perspective on how damaging negative thoughts can really be, we're going to address some science in this chapter. Our genetic code can be changed by negative thinking and even be passed on to our kids. But all hope is not lost, as we will end by discussing how gratitude can be an antidote for keeping a healthy perspective and a sound mind-set.

EPIGENETICS

The term epigenetics is defined as the study of changes in organisms caused by the modification of gene expression rather than the alteration of the genetic code itself.[16]

In 2013, a groundbreaking study showed that trauma gets passed down from generation to generation.[17] The study was out to prove that fear and traumatic events can impact generations to come. Male mice were used in the study to ensure genetic connection instead of nurture. These males were exposed to the scent of acetophenone, which is described as "the smell of orange blossom with a hint of cherry."

At the same time the smell was released, the experimenters sent a mild shock through the wires the mice were standing on, which caused pain. This was replicated over the course

---

16   Sarah Green. "Epigenetics."
17   Brian G. Dias and Kerry J. Ressler. "Parental Olfactory Experience Influences Behavior and Neural Structure in Subsequent Generations." (89)

of three days, then a ten-day waiting period before the mice were allowed to mate.

When the offspring of these mice were exposed to the acetophenone scent, the pups experienced a noticeable reaction of fear. The researchers took it a step further and artificially inseminated the next generation to ensure that the male mice didn't pass genetic code on during mating. The same results were duplicated.

Alcohol and other scents similar to acetophenone were used that produced no reaction in the pups. Something related to that fear was passed down via sperm alone, generations beyond the first. Many similar findings have been reported in humans—specifically pregnant mothers who developed PTSD after surviving September 11, 2001, and the offspring of those mothers.[18]

So traumatic and negative reactions seem to get passed down from generation to generation, but little evidence that positive mental health traits get passed down. It's not to say that they don't, but negative ones seem to trump the positive based on everything I have seen. This makes things like practicing gratitude all that more critical to maintain sound mental health.

---

18 Rachel Yehuda, et. al. "Transgenerational Effects of Posttraumatic Stress Disorder in Babies of Mothers Exposed to the World Trade Center Attacks during Pregnancy." (4115)

PLAYING ROULETTE

In 2017, Facebook founders admitted to creating a platform that played on human addiction and exploited that knowledge for the purpose of profit and growth.[19] Most people agree that access to addictive substances should be banned for children, but what about social media?

Dr. Zubin Damania is the founder and CEO of Turntable Health, a primary care clinic that was funded by Zappos' CEO Tony Hsieh. Damania is a healthcare innovator known by his alter ego, ZDoggMD. He uses satire, music, and humor to reach people about health issues. After entering medicine to help as many people as he could, he would look into the mirror and feel at times like a zombie. Both of his parents were doctors, but his parents warned him that the medical system was broken, and doctors were not incentivized to help people but to do things to people—surgeries and procedures were the most profitable.

Even with this warning, he chose to pursue a medical career and soon noticed he was in for more than he bargained for.

"Medical school is a lot like Hogwarts…once we emerged, we were not muggles anymore," Damania says in his *TEDMED* talk.[20]

He describes the stress of ten years in primary practice as a rush and race all day from patient to paperwork to insurance

---

19   Mike Allen. "Sean Parker Unloads on Facebook: 'God Only Knows What It's Doing to Our Children's Brains.'"

20   Zubin Damania. "Are Zombie Doctors Taking over America?"

and repeat, just to end the day with so much worry that he missed something critical for one of his patients.

"By the time we arrive at our destination as a practicing doctor, it's so abhorrent to who we really are, but we can't stop playing the game… a shuffling zombie denial."

He couldn't be a zombie any longer and chose to go the YouTube route with a fellow colleague to reach people in an alternative way.

His delivery mechanism may be alternative, but Damania is connecting and helping far more people than he ever could have imagined as a practicing internal medicine doctor. He moved to Las Vegas and took a risk starting Turntable Health. The point of the clinic was to disrupt the broken health care system by not using the standard fee-for-service model.

He developed a model that could change the health care industry, hoping that fixing primary care will eventually upend the insurance nightmare that exists right now. He aimed to help and enable the patient rather than doing things to them just to maximize profit. Though insurance companies could not get on board and Turntable Health was forced to close its doors in 2017, Damania didn't let it get him down.

"It sounds cliché (and it is), but you need to reconnect with that unique part of yourself that has gifts to give the world."

In one of his recent YouTube messages[21] about what social media is doing to our daughters, he cuts out all the theatrics,

---

21 ZdoggMD. "What Is Social Media Doing to Our Daughters?"

growing serious because he doesn't want anything to be over-looked. As a father of two daughters, Damania projects an intensity that contrasts his normal light and airy tone. He prefaces that if you have girls, you need to pay attention, because an alarming trend in girls born after 1994 is sur-facing—this group of girls has a notable increase in anxiety and depression and a significantly sharp increase in suicide.

Damania goes on to cite Greg Lukianoff and Jonathan Haidt in their book *The Coddling of the American Mind*. The authors acknowledge this alarming trend and state that parents are too overprotective and not letting kids take risks, which is keeping kids fragile by sheltering them from adver-sity. These kids fall apart when adversity does eventually hit. He says this is just one piece of the pie. The much bigger piece is what each of us carries around in our pockets with us every day—our smartphones. In a dramatic tone, Damania claims this is as deadly as carrying a handgun, because "we have weaponized something that is so dangerous to young girls … social media."

Damania has compiled data that suggests that young boys are physically aggressive—they bully, hit, and punch. "If you gave every young boy a handgun in this country, there would be an epidemic of violence, because they are impulsive and take things out physically." Young girls are "just as aggressive but it's a different kind called social aggression." This in the past was done at school, in cliques or out, but you could go home and be safe again. But now with smartphones, and when using particular social media platforms, it is constant. These girls have no escape from the bullying, name-calling, and reputation tarnishing.

The FOMO (fear of missing out) has now become so critical to young girls' lives, and it's all played out via social media where they can now see if they were not invited to a social event and it's thrown in their faces. Damania calls these direct relational attacks, the equivalent of gunfire to their emotional well-being, with nowhere to hide and be safe. When this is combined with being sheltered, they are at critical risk for a mental health crisis. "There is absolutely no upside and every potential downside."

What is his recommendation? No access to social media at all until high school is over. He has committed that his daughters will not access social media until that point in time, and that he will work on teaching them about handling adversity and taking calculated risks.

I would argue that boys can be just as affected but tend not to show it like girls. So what is the point, and where does gratitude tie in? Social media is here to stay, and kids are using it. Banning it may be just as traumatic as allowing them free rein, given this FOMO phenomenon, so what can be done? We need the perspective of gratitude more than ever and providing a safe zone within the family where kids can share and be vulnerable without judgment is just as crucial.

THE POWER OF THOUGHTS

It's been known for some time that positive and negative thought patterns can affect our health accordingly, but evidence suggests that thoughts can affect your body on a cellular level. Dr. Masaru Emoto believed that emotional energy or vibrations could change the physical structure of water, and his published books, including *The Hidden Messages in Water*, show ice crystals that formed when attached to certain negative or positive words or thoughts. His experiments go beyond his own laboratories, as peer-reviewed studies were also performed.

The resulting ice crystals were amazing. Formations that emerged from positive words, thoughts, or emotions were beautiful symmetrical shapes, while negative words, thoughts, or emotions created distorted crystals. This was taken a step further to determine if thoughts could travel to water in another location.

An experiment titled "Double-Blind Test of the Effects of Distant Intention on Water Crystal Formation" was done at the Institute of Noetic Sciences.[22]

The hypothesis that water treated with intention can affect ice crystals got serious attention from the scientific community due to the results of this experiment when the water was pilot tested under double-blind conditions.

A group of approximately two thousand people in Tokyo focused positive thoughts toward water samples located inside an electromagnetically shielded room in California. Remarkably, only certain kinds of formations were present within the water they were concentrating on, even though ice crystals formed in both water sample sets. The group was unaware of similar water samples set aside in a different location as controls.

---

22   Dean Radin, et al. "Double-Blind Test of the Effects of Distant Intention on Water Crystal Formation." (408)

"Ice crystals formed from both sets of water samples were blindly identified and photographed by an analyst, and the resulting images were blindly assessed for aesthetic appeal by one hundred independent judges. Results indicated that crystals from the treated water were given higher scores for aesthetic appeal than those from the control water (P = .001, one-tailed), lending support to the hypothesis," concluded the team led by Dr. Dean Radin.

Again, the same amazing results were duplicated. While some try to poke holes in Dr. Emoto's first studies, it's hard to argue with a double-blind, peer-reviewed study, as this is the gold standard when trying to prove efficacy for every new drug that comes through the pharmaceutical pipeline. If the power of positive and negative thoughts can have this effect on water forming into ice crystals, how can they affect all the cells in our body, and what can these thoughts do (positively or negatively) to us on a cellular level?

The crystals formed with "Thank You" and "Love and Gratitude" are not an anomaly—these thoughts do transform our bodies. When I meditate with gratitude intertwined in prayer, I often think of these beautiful crystals and my negative thoughts and feelings transforming from something repulsive into something as beautiful.

"Finally, brothers and sisters, whatever is true, whatever is noble, whatever is right, whatever is pure, whatever is lovely, whatever is admirable—if anything is excellent or praiseworthy—think about such things."

PHILIPPIANS 4:8 NIV

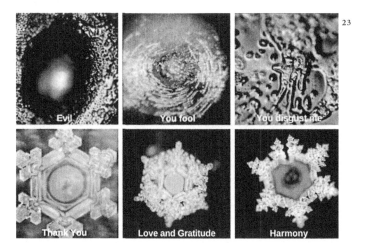

Evil | You fool | You disgust me
Thank You | Love and Gratitude | Harmony

"People do not decide to become extraordinary. They decide to accomplish extraordinary things."

—EDMUND HILLARY

THOUGHTS TRANSFORMED INTO REALITY

Anthony (Tony) J. Mahavoric was born on February 29, 1960, in North Hollywood, California. His mother struggled with alcohol and prescription drug addiction, and he had to find work as a handyman when he was very young to help support his siblings. One Thanksgiving when he was eleven, his family had no money or food to celebrate with, and he was given a turkey. He realized that some strangers did care, when he had been told his whole life that nobody did. That simple act of kindness resonated with him at that young age, and he

23   Masaru Emoto. *The Hidden Messages in Water.* (91-137)

decided that he wanted to make that kind of difference in others' lives as best he could.[24]

In high school, he decided he needed to set goals to become successful, rich, and to be able to help others. He set a goal to read a book a day as a sophomore. While he didn't quite hit that goal, he did read seven hundred books in seven years, and from then on mapped out his goals. He planned each decade of his life based on what he wanted to achieve—in his twenties he would help individual people; in his thirties, small groups; then in his forties, large groups and organizations; and, finally, society. Tony changed his last name to "Robbins," which was his father's surname.

At seventeen, while working as a mover, he asked his father's friend, a landlord, this question: "My dad says you used to be such a loser, and how come you're so successful now?"

The landlord credited a seminar he took with Jim Rohn for turning his life around. Robbins then asked his father's friend if he could get him into the seminar, and he said he could but would not, because Robbins would squander the opportunity.

Probing further, Tony found out that a seminar would cost him a full week's pay, but he made the decision to invest in himself that day, saved up, and attended his first Jim Rohn seminar, which changed the trajectory of his life. Rohn was known as one of the pioneer motivational speakers, sharing his philosophies after achieving much success in business. Many credit Rohn with influencing them at an early point

---

24   Robert Lewis. "Tony Robbins."

in their lives, including successful motivational speakers like Jack Canfield and Brian Tracy.[25]

Robbins says, "He taught me that if you want anything to change, you must change. If you want things to get better, you've got to get better. And that the secret to life is working harder on myself than on the job, skill, or anything else. Rohn taught me that as soon as I committed myself to excellence, I would really have something to give others."

Furthermore, Rohn taught Robbins that the emotions of gratitude, courage, faith, determination, compassion, and love must be fed and nurtured continuously because "weeds in our garden are automatic," "inevitable," and we must "stand guard at the door of our mind, feeding it with knowledge and thoughts that empower" us. Rohn passed away in 2009, and Robbins spoke at his funeral.[26]

Robbins saw people spending more than five years in therapy and still not feeling whole, which he thought was absurd. He decided to apply the seminar approach to problems, with a focus on maximizing resources and results, and things took off for him from there. He made his first million at twenty-four. Two years later, he wrote the book *Unlimited Power*, and the success of his empire snowballed after that. Although he is most known for being a speaker and coach, he has amassed a business conglomerate—from asteroid mining to 3D-printed prosthetics—bringing in over $6 billion in revenue annually.

---

25   Richard Feloni. "Tony Robbins Started out as a Broke Janitor—Then He Saved a Week's Worth of Pay, and the Way He Spent It Changed His Life."
26   Tony Robbins. "The Mentors Who Coached Me."

He also has several philanthropic endeavors, including Feeding America on Thanksgiving each year, which he has intentionally grown exponentially through the years, now providing millions of meals. He also founded Give Something Back, which has been implemented in schools, prisons, service organizations, and shelters.

In addition to his mentoring and hard work, Robbins credits a ten-minute daily routine[27] that he faithfully practices to his overwhelming success. Robbins begins each day with gratitude, stating that it's the most important ten minutes to each day and brings more success into his life. Not only does he express gratitude during this ritual, but he makes an effort to feel it, stating "you can't be fearful, anxious, depressed, and grateful at the same time," so he creates a powerful mind-set shift to offset these common negative emotions.

Robbins says, "So if you want to conquer those emotions, maybe it's time to train your nervous system to go into gratitude more naturally."

"For as he thinks within himself, so he is."

PROVERBS 23:7 NASB

PUTTING IT INTO PRACTICE

During his short routine, Robbins takes the three following steps:

---

27   Tom Huddleston, Jr. "This Is Tony Robbins's 10-Minute Morning Routine to 'Change Your Day for the Better.'"

1. He focuses on something simple that makes him feel grateful, like the wind in his face or a child's smile.
2. He devotes three minutes to prayer, and during this time, he sends energy to his friends, family, coworkers, and others.
3. He completes "three to thrive," taking the last three minutes of his routine to identify three results he's committed to achieving.

Robbins says that taking these few moments each day are key and manageable for anyone at any age or stage in their career. No one has an excuse. It's not a coincidence that his whole routine is launched by gratitude. "Change your expectations for appreciation, and the world changes instantly."

When asked about his failures, Robbins says he has made millions, and he tries to learn something each and every time. However, when asked about his fears, he states he doesn't have any. "Gratitude is the solution to anger and fear."

Robbins illustrates his point with the story of a beginning skier going over the edge to find they're on a black diamond. If you're that skier, what do you do next? Do you go into fear mode and try to not get hurt and play it safe, or do you try as best as you can with the skills you have to face it head on?

Facing your challenges is the way to tackle each fear in your life, according to Robbins, and each time you conquer a fear, you grow more and more fearless.[28]

---

28 Richard Feloni. "Tony Robbins Gives Every Entrepreneur the Same Two Pieces of Advice."

I really like how Tony Robbins spells out a formula for conquering fear, anxiety, and depression through gratitude. Robbins has been successful for decades, but he still devotes ten minutes every day to keep gratitude at the forefront of his perspective. If we don't keep it in practice, its benefits diminish. In Chapter 9, we will explore further ways to cultivate gratitude on a regular basis.

"'Who has known the mind of the Lord so as to instruct him?' But we have the mind of Christ."

1 CORINTHIANS 2:16 NIV

CHAPTER 4

PHYSICAL HEALTH

——

"Something as simple as moving into a state of joy, love, or gratitude for five to ten minutes a day can produce significant epigenetic changes in our health and bodies."

—DR. JOE DISPENZA

AWAKENING

Joe Dispenza was completing the bike portion of a triathlon in 1986 at age twenty-three in Palm Springs, California, when he came upon an intersection. At that moment, a Chevy Bronco traveling 55 mph whose driver didn't see him collided with the rear of his bike, catapulting Dispenza into the air.

The impact compressed six vertebrae, broke his back in four places, and left shattered bone fragments in his spinal cord. His best option was a surgery called the Harrington Rod procedure where the spine would be fused by a rod from base to neck, which included an incredibly long, painful recovery period. Worse yet, his odds of walking again were bleak, even with the best possible surgical outcome.[29]

Dispenza says, "In order for some of us to wake up, we need a wake-up call."

Surprisingly, he turned down surgery and checked out of the hospital, thinking, "the power that made the body heals the body." In his mind, he would spend three or more hours a day mentally reconstructing his spine vertebra by vertebra, but then he would think of living in a wheelchair and derail all his envisioned progress.

---

29 Dr. Joe Dispenza. "How I Healed Myself After Breaking 6 Vertebrae."

Dispenza went through this mental torment for six weeks, frustrated that he couldn't get his mind to do what he wanted it to. But he stuck with it, over three hours each day, and by the end of that six weeks, he was able to go through his whole spine without distraction—and then it clicked.[30]

"It felt like I'd hit the sweet spot of a tennis ball," he recalled.

He started noticing significant changes in his body. His motor functions began to return, and his body began to heal and change. Within ten weeks, he was on his feet again, then walking and getting even stronger, and finally training again at twelve weeks. During his darkest moments, he made a deal with himself that if he was ever able to walk again, he would spend the rest of his life studying the mind/body connection and the mind over matter conundrum. From 1986 onward, he has done exactly that, authoring three books and helping thousands of others heal and become aware of the power of our minds through his books and workshops. Dispenza is one of the thought leaders today in neuroplasticity.

CONNECTING THE MIND AND THE BODY

Dispenza has dissected his miraculous recovery to come up with a formula that he teaches to others: clear intention plus elevated emotion equals the desired outcome. Using this formula, he was able to heal fully from his catastrophic accident, even though doctors told him his odds of life outside a wheelchair were slim to none. What would have happened if he had succumbed to that diagnosis?

---

30   London Real. "DR JOE DISPENZA—HOW I HEALED MYSELF | London Real."

Cognitive neuroscientist Dr. Caroline Leaf adds, "By the same token, if you choose to add a signal—for example, saying something like, 'My mother had depression and that's why I have depression, and now my daughter is suffering from depression'—then the epigenetic markers are activated. The thinking and speaking out the problem serve as the signal that makes it a reality." She continues, "Research shows that seventy-five to ninety-eight percent of mental, physical, and behavioral illness comes from one's thought life."[31]

Could this be why so many of us are plagued by ailments that will not heal? Perhaps at some point we were "diagnosed" into a bucket and have mentally accepted that reality. I don't think it's a coincidence that since our society has become more stressed and mentally taxed beyond what we can handle, our rates of autoimmune disorders, anxiety, depression, and sleep issues have skyrocketed. Research indicates that seventy-five to ninety percent of all visits to primary care physicians are for stress-related issues.[32]

I believe this is what happened to me—my wake-up call. I thought I was chugging along just fine, but my life kept adding "balls" I had to keep in the air all at once, like an extreme juggler you might see at Cirque du Soleil. Without even realizing it, I hit a breaking point, and my body started to shut down. It's hard not to think about all the lost years with my young children, but I choose to focus on the positive and the fact that my health journey brought me to where I am now: stronger, more appreciative of God's grace, grateful for all

---

31 Caroline Leaf. *Switch on Your Brain: The Key to Peak Happiness, Thinking, and Health.*

32 "The Effects of Stress on Your Body."

I have, and with a new perspective to help others through what I learned.

During his workshops, Dispenza teaches his meditation practices and empowers others to use their minds to heal themselves. "We've seen gene changes in four days...seen people with MS heal in two days," Dispenza exclaims in his book, *Breaking the Habit of Being Yourself.* "Thoughts are the vocabulary of the brain. Feelings are the vocabulary of the body."

Dispenza's incredible insight is backed up by much scientific research. Thoughts and feelings are so integral to both physical and mental health, and when we make that connection, putting them together, we can morph into our optimal selves. So what feeling does Dr. Dispenza believe is the most powerful? Big surprise—it's gratitude.

GRATITUDE AND IMMUNE HEALTH

Dispenza wanted to prove the power of elevated emotions, so he taught one of his advanced workshops in Tacoma, Washington, near his home. "We performed a study on gratitude whereby we took 120 people and measured their cortisol and IgA levels at the start and conclusion of the workshop," he explains in his blog entry entitled *The Power of Gratitude.*[33]

Cortisol is a stress hormone. When we live in this constant state of fight-or-flight, it uses an exorbitant amount of our body's energy. That energy gets pulled from other functions like the immune response. "In other words, if we are utilizing

---

33   Dr. Joe Dispenza. *The Power of Gratitude.*

all the body's resources for some threat in our outer world, there is little energy in our inner world for growth, repair, and internal defense. Thus, the lower our immune system, the more susceptible we are to sickness and disease," Dispenza says.

He goes on to explain that as cortisol levels go up, a chemical called IgA, also produced in direct relation to cortisol, decreases. This scenario isn't good because IgA is necessary for immunity and one of the strongest building blocks we have. Dispenza states, "IgA is responsible for the healthy function of our…immune system. It's constantly fighting a barrage of bacteria, viruses, and organisms that invade and/or are already living within the body's internal environment." He adds, "IgA is better than any flu shot or immune system booster you could possibly take—and it's totally natural."

Over the course of the four-day workshop, Dispenza asked all 120 study participants to shift into an elevated emotional state (love, joy, or gratitude) for approximately ten minutes, three times a day. He was looking to prove that if we could elevate our emotional states, we could raise our immune system and reduce the production of negative stress hormones like cortisol. "We discovered at the conclusion of the event that the cortisol levels of our participants dropped by three standard deviations, and their IgA levels shot up on average from 52.5 to 86 [mg/dl]." These are significant changes, and although the study wasn't set up with a control group, it's evident that an emotion such as gratitude can have a dramatic effect on our physical health.

I find this study profound. Our thoughts coupled with our emotions can not only heal but prime our body for optimal health.

"What this tells us is that we don't need a pharmacy or an exogenous substance to heal us," Dispenza says. "We have the power from within to upregulate the genes that make IgA. Something as simple as moving into an elevated state of joy, love, or gratitude for five to ten minutes a day can produce significant epigenetic changes in our health and bodies."

Dispenza has much more fascinating research and outcomes that he shares in his books, including why gratitude—as opposed to joy and love—is the most powerful emotional state, and we will come back to his studies in Chapter 8.

GRATITUDE AND DNA

Dr. Bruce Lipton, who has extensively studied quantum physics and epigenetics, states that gratitude is essential to our well-being and goes on to break it down to a cellular level in his video *The Healing Power of Gratitude—Bruce Lipton Explains Telomeres*. He explains in great detail the science of healthy and aging cells in relation to the telomeres at the ends of DNA strands.

According to Lipton, telomeres appear to have no function except to add length to DNA strands. Each time a cell duplicates and the DNA is replicated, the enzyme responsible for duplication reads the strand until just shy of the end, and some is cut off each time. If the strand has long enough telomeres at the ends of the DNA strands, the chromosomes won't be disturbed, and aging won't happen at an accelerated speed.

The average person has enough telomeres to live approximately 120 years, which is in line with the human lifespan as we know it today. An enzyme called telomerase can extend the telomeres at the end of a DNA strand, and scientists have researched what directly causes increases and decreases of telomerase in a person.

Poor nutrition, childhood abuse, domestic violence, PTSD, lack of love for oneself or love from others, isolation, and lack of purpose can all decrease telomerase. On the contrary, good nutrition, exercise, happiness, gratitude, a positive outlook, self-love, and serving others can all increase telomerase. Of these, Dr. Lipton emphasizes gratitude as the most powerful, as our minds can thus influence our cells to be healthier and live longer.[34]

"We are not victims of our genes but masters of our fates, able to create lives overflowing with peace, happiness, and love," Lipton states.

When I look at the positive attributes of increased telomerase, I would have to agree with Dr. Lipton—practicing gratitude also increases happiness and a will to help others, therefore catalyzing four of the factors that increase the enzyme needed for healthy cell life.

---

34 Bruce H. Lipton. *The Healing Power of Gratitude—Bruce Lipton Explains Telomeres.*

MIND AND MUSCLE STRENGTH

In 2014, researchers at the Ohio Musculoskeletal and Neuro-logical Institute (OMNI) at Ohio University set up a study to show that the power of thought can help to maintain muscle strength following a period of immobilization in a cast.

For this study, fifteen subjects were asked to wear a rigid cast that extended from below the elbow to just past the tips of the fingers for a total of four weeks. This prevented the hand and wrist from moving. As a control group, fifteen subjects did not wear a cast. Of those who did wear the immobilizing cast on their wrists and hands, half of them engaged in a mental imagery exercise that required them to picture that they were contracting their wrists for five seconds and resting for five seconds afterward—four times in a row, with a one-minute break, for thirteen rounds that occurred five times per week. Their imagination was guided with these instructions:

"Begin imagining that you are pushing in as hard as you can with your left wrist. Push, push, push…and stop."

No imagery exercises were provided to the second group.

After the four-week experiment was over, both of the casted groups had lost strength in their casted limbs when com-pared to the control group. However, the group that per-formed the mental exercises lost fifty percent less strength than the group who didn't complete the exercises. The muscle strength lost was twenty-four percent in the imagery group and forty-five percent in the non-imagery group. In addition to this, voluntary activation (VA), or the nervous system's ability to fully activate the muscle, was much quicker in the imagery group in comparison to those who didn't practice imagery.[35]

A study published in *Personality and Individual Differences* in 2012[36] demonstrated that grateful people reported feeling healthier, exercised more often, and had fewer aches and pains than people who didn't practice gratitude. Those who were grateful also reported taking better care of their health and attending regular doctors' visits. These habits are likely to contribute to a longer lifespan.

GENETICS VERSUS MIND-SET

Nikki first heard the words "breast cancer" when she was nineteen years old, when her aunt Sue was diagnosed. It wasn't until later that those words really hit home when her aunt Katherine, her maternal grandmother, and then her mom were all diagnosed. In 2006, not long after her mother was diagnosed, Nikki recalls making the family genetic connection. Many emotions set in—including anger and terror. Due to her genetic predisposition at that time, she made the brave decision to have a preventative mastectomy in 2010.

In 2015, when her mother was fighting breast cancer and after her own mastectomy, Nikki remembers shopping with her for some new clothes that would fit. What should have been a relaxing afternoon of bonding turned into an afternoon of

---

35 American Physiological Society (APS). "Mind over Matter: Can You Think Your Way to Strength?"

36 Patrick L. Hill, Mathias Allemand, and Brent W. Roberts. "Examining the Pathways Between Gratitude and Self-Rated Physical Health Across Adulthood." (92)

despair. They went from store to store as her mother tried on a multitude of clothes. None of them fit properly or made her feel beautiful. Her mom, normally so strong and always there to help others regardless of her own struggles, was in pain, feeling like less of a woman. This broke Nikki's heart.

She knew she needed to do something to help her mother, and she made a promise that day to design and make clothes to help women who have been through this radical surgery feel beautiful again. Her mom did not get to see this come to fruition, as she passed away shortly after, but Nikki kept her promise. She took her pain and sorrow and helped other people. It was during this time that she found gratitude and realized what her mom had known all along.

"When you reach down below your pain and struggles, you find a way to be helpful to other people," recalls Nikki, which is exactly what her mom had always exemplified. "You find a purpose, passion, and reason to continue on day after day and be happy." Nikki cites gratitude as welling up from the heart, a gift from her mother and the catalyst that enabled her to stop being angry and start helping others.

In addition to her mind-set shift, she saw her marriage and children change. Nikki shared a story. When her children would come to her late at night, complaining about how they weren't able to sleep, she recalls sounding like a broken record, saying, "Go back to bed, and as you lay there, think of all the things you are grateful for."

The next morning, without exception, they would come to her and tell her, "You're right, mom, it works every time. I just need to lay there and be thankful for all I have." Just like that, they would fall asleep.

"I'm so grateful I had a mom who was a strong woman, strong in her faith. Now I can be more like her, giving to others in her name, blessing as many as I can," Nikki gushed.

Nikki's story shows how a blessing can come from the deepest of pains. Finding gratitude at that low point and changing her perspective led her to help others. Nikki found a purpose in her deepest sorrow and pain. And she says, day after day, "I get to wake up and do this!" She recounts almost having to pinch herself at how blessed she's been to be led down this path, amazed by how something so beautiful could grow out of something so painful and sorrowful, something to help other people.

The groundbreaking studies connecting mind and body will hopefully one day eliminate the need for preventative mastectomies. But for now, I have no doubt that Nikki's physical health has greatly benefited from her mental state as she continues to live free of cancer in gratitude day after day.

GRATITUDE AND SLEEP

Psychologists Dr. Robert Emmons and Dr. Michael McCullough asked people who suffered from neuromuscular disorders to practice gratitude nightly by making a list of things they were grateful for. The participants followed up after three weeks, at which time they reported feeling more refreshed and sleeping longer. Researchers at the University of Manchester in England continued the study of gratitude and sleep by putting together a study of four hundred adults of all ages. Forty percent of this group had sleep disorders. They were asked to practice gratitude at bedtime and reported having more positive thoughts and fewer negative ones. This correlated with falling asleep faster and better with longer sleep times.[37]

The Bible in 1 Corinthians 12:12 and 12:14–27 NIV, does a great job explaining that the body and mind aren't disconnected. Not only are all our body parts connected, but we are connected to each other. I couldn't have said it any better.

> Just as a body, though one, has many parts, but all its many parts form one body, so it is with Christ…. Even so the body is not made up of one part but of many.
>
> Now if the foot should say, "Because I am not a hand, I do not belong to the body," it would not for that reason stop being part of the body…. If the whole body were an eye, where would the sense of hearing be? If the whole body were an ear, where would the sense of smell be? But in fact God has placed the parts in the body, every one of them, just as he wanted them to be. If they were all one part, where would the body be? As it is, there are many parts, but one body.
>
> The eye cannot say to the hand, "I don't need you!" And the head cannot say to the feet, "I don't need you!" On the contrary, those parts of the body that seem to be weaker

---

37   Robert A. Emmons, Michael E. McCullough. "Counting Blessings vs. Burdens: An Experimental Investigation of Gratitude and Subjective Well-Being in Daily Life." (377-389)

are indispensable, and the parts that we think are less honorable we treat with special honor. And the parts that are unpresentable are treated with special modesty, while our presentable parts need no special treatment. But God has put the body together, giving greater honor to the parts that lacked it, so that there should be no division in the body, but that its parts should have equal concern for each other. If one part suffers, every part suffers with it; if one part is honored, every part rejoices with it.

Now you are the body of Christ, and each one of you is a part of it.

So we have the body of Christ and the mind of Christ—what obstacles could stand in our way? The power of our thoughts goes way beyond our mental state to affect our physical health in profound ways.

PUTTING IT INTO PRACTICE

As demonstrated by Dr. Dispenza, visualization is an important component in physical recovery. Visualization coupled with the most powerful emotion—gratitude—can put your physical health on the fast track to recovery.

Think of something that is physically "off" right now. Start with something minor. Perhaps you have an ache or a pulled muscle that's been nagging you.

First, come up with a memory or thought of something that brings instant joy. Now embrace the gratitude you feel for that moment or thought and concentrate on that feeling.

With that feeling strong in your head, bring in your ailment and visualize its absence while keeping the feeling of gratitude strong in your senses. This takes practice and may need to be repeated several times to see results.

CHAPTER 5

ABILITY TO HANDLE ADVERSITY

———

"The struggle ends when gratitude begins."

—NEALE DONALD WALSCH

UNEXPECTED TRAGEDY

Sheryl Sandberg is most known for her current role as the COO of Facebook and has received many accolades for the company's success. Her early life is obscure—she grew up in Washington, DC, then moved to Florida and attended North Miami Beach High School. After graduating from Harvard, Sandberg didn't initially seem to be heading in the tech direction and instead became the deputy secretary treasurer for the Clinton administration.

She briefly married Brian Kraff in 1993—which lasted only a year—and she chalks that up as being young and not knowing what she wanted. Later she would say, "Who you marry is the single most important career decision you can make."

Interestingly, Sandberg made the jump from politics to Silicon Valley in 2000. It took her ten months to find a job. While she eventually took a position at Google as vice president of global online sales and operations, she almost went to another unnamed company if it weren't for the keen advice of her friend Eric Schmidt: "If you are offered a seat on a rocket ship, don't ask what seat. Just get on!"

A few years later, in 2004, she met and married Dave Goldberg, and soon after they had their first child together.

At a holiday cocktail party in 2007, she met Mark Zuckerberg for the first time. To say that meeting went well would be an understatement. They not only hit it off personally but professionally, as Zuckerberg was impressed with her intelligence. Remembering the advice of Schmidt, she accepted a job as the COO of Facebook in 2008. From that point on, things seemed to be skyrocketing for Sandberg, and her notoriety grew exponentially. Facebook had a $56 million loss the year she came on board, but in the following eight years, the company grew sixty-five times to nearly $3.7 billion in profit.

Sandberg admits to being blissfully happy during this time in her life. She and her husband Dave, who was the CEO of SurveyMonkey, both lived in the Silicon Valley royalty circle of privilege and influence. In 2015, Sandberg and her husband were vacationing in Mexico with friends and family. She was tired and decided to take a nap.

Not much later, she woke and her husband Dave wasn't there. She and Dave's brother searched for him and found him in the gym next to an elliptical machine. His face was blue and his head was lying in a small pool of blood. They administered CPR until the ambulance arrived. Dave was pronounced dead at the hospital, and the cause of death was arrhythmia.

Sandberg had to return home to her kids, delivering the news that their father was gone forever. She became a shell of grief, admitting to not knowing someone could "cry so much so often." At the advice of psychologists, she returned to her and the kids' schedule just ten days later.[38]

"Dave's death changed me in profound ways," she says. "I learned about the depths of sadness and the brutality of loss. But I also learned that when life sucks you under, you can kick against the bottom, break the surface, and breathe again."

Even though I walk through the valley of the shadow of death,

I will fear no evil,
for you are with me;
your rod and your staff,
they comfort me.

                                                        PSALM 23:4 ESV

She confided in Adam Grant (psychologist, author, and professor at Wharton) and shared that her "greatest fear was that my kids would never be happy again." She had met Grant four years earlier at dinner in their home—her husband had read his book *Give and Take* and had asked him to come speak to his company. Grant asked Sandberg a seemingly heartless question at the time that proved pivotal in her ability to build resilience and get through the grief: "You should think about how things could be worse." He continued, "Well, Dave could have had that same cardiac arrhythmia while driving the children."[39]

---

38 Decca Aitkenhead. "Sheryl Sandberg: 'Everyone Looked at Me like I Was a Ghost.'"
39 Ari Shapiro. "'Just Show Up': Sheryl Sandberg On How To Help Someone Who's Grieving."

It was at that moment that Sandberg felt something other than grief: gratitude. This was a pivotal realization for her. "To this day, when I need it, I think about that," Sandberg said. "I sit here today, and I am sadder, but I appreciate life in a way I never did before. What if it had been worse?"

In 2016, in her commencement speech to UC Berkeley, Sandberg wrapped up with these poignant words: "It is the greatest irony of my life that losing my husband helped me find deeper gratitude—gratitude for the kindness of my friends, the love of my family, the laughter of my children. My hope for you is that you can find that gratitude—not just on the good days, like today, but on the hard ones, when you will really need it."[40]

Sandberg would later quote, "'I've never known anyone who was only given roses.'"

I almost need to take a step back to take that in, even after studying and practicing gratitude for years. It still seems counterintuitive to find gratitude and appreciation in the worst situations, and an impossible feat as well. But I can attest to what Sandberg says. If you take the worst situations and find the smallest blessing in the pain, loss, heartache, or oppression, you take back control. What blossoms from that small feeling of gratitude will truly amaze you.

I find it brave and admirable of Sandberg to be so vulnerable and share her journey to help others find their way out of the darkness using gratitude. She went through an unthinkable

---

40 Meghan O'Dea. "Transcript: Sheryl Sandberg at the University of California at Berkeley 2016 Commencement."

loss but emerged on the other side of life again—with pain, yes, but with stronger resilience for the next curveball life throws her way.

"Finding gratitude and appreciation is key to resilience. People who take the time to list things they are grateful for are happier and healthier," Sandberg exclaims.

"I have told you these things, so that in me you may have peace. In this world you will have trouble. But take heart! I have overcome the world."

JOHN 16:33 NIV

LOSING IT ALL

Matthew Maher was born in 1984 in Cape May Court House on the southern tip of New Jersey near the ocean, one of four boys to a loving Christian family. Like his brothers, he excelled in athletics, realizing early on that soccer was his sport. He enjoyed much success and was awarded a scholarship to play at Temple University. Shortly after graduating in 2007, he went to North Carolina to visit his brother Anthony, who was playing professional soccer there, and was able to practice and hang out with the team.

He was soon given his own contract to play on that same team alongside his brother—his dream not only realized but magnified with family. His first start as a professional was against Mexican powerhouse Cruz Azul.

Maher describes how surreal it felt to be on the same field playing against one of his childhood heroes and hearing the crowd cheering for him.

In March 2009, he took a routine turn on the turf during a game and tore the meniscus in his knee, which is hard to recover from and play again at a professional level. He traveled with the team in May 2009 to Baltimore on the injured reserve list and remembers being in a mental haze, thinking of his looming surgery in the coming week to repair his knee. Maher decided to go out for the night without a plan to distract himself. He went into a bar where the bartender knew his brother, gave his condolences for his knee injury, and set up a line of shots on the house for the group he was with.

Without telling the group about the free drinks, he took at least five of the shots himself. The next thing he remembers were the lights coming on and the bar closing. On a whim, he and a friend decided to drive to Atlantic City about twenty miles away. He remembers driving much too fast, 85–90 mph, and changing lanes with a quick look over his shoulder. A jolting impact with another vehicle sent his SUV spinning and rolling before finally coming to a stop.

He recalls being cuffed and receiving multiple breathalyzer tests, which all confirmed his inebriated state. While in the holding cell, Maher remembers a muffled voice over dispatch that he craned his neck to hear through the bars of his cell, listening to the words that he will never forget.

"Driver in the black Escalade is in custody."

A long, painful pause followed as he remembers trying with every ounce of his being to understand the words coming through the muffled speaker.

"Driver in the Town and Country is deceased."

Those words hit Maher like a brick wall, followed by denial of what they meant, followed by the pain they brought onto everyone in his and his victim's lives—all the lives that would never be the same again.

The court day was emotional to say the least, but one of the most beautiful recollections of the deceased Hort Kap was his daughter's testimony. She spoke of her dad's legacy—that he was an immigrant, father of six, and a hard worker. The joy that she remembered him with was felt throughout the room. Then his son, Noon, got up to share a gut-wrenching recollection of the moment he found out about his father's death.

"Do you have any idea how I found out about my daddy dying?" Noon choked out as he pointed at Maher. He proceeded to take the courtroom through the horrid night in detail, ending his emotional journey by locking eyes with Maher and whispering, "And you destroyed my world."

With a pause that felt like an eternity as eyes were being wiped and sniffles were heard through the room, Noon's final words came unexpectedly.

"But I forgive you, my brother."

Noon came over, and they embraced like brothers as Maher cried, "I'm so sorry," in his ear.

"January 7, 2010," Maher remembered. "The exact day I was sentenced to five and a half years in prison was the day I was set free."

The gratitude Maher felt at that moment, along with the undeserved forgiveness he was given, was what changed him inside. After realizing the gravity of a decision that resulted in someone else's death, grasping the ripple effect upon so many people was overwhelming.

He can't fully describe or put into words the extent of the humiliation, shame, and embarrassment he felt. But in that one moment, it was all changed. Before the incident, he put his identity in the world and believed in his job security and his talent. All that had been stripped away, and he was so grateful to feel the forgiveness of his victim's son and the forgiveness of God. Alongside the support of family around him, he felt the goodness of God and overwhelming gratitude for all he had.

Three years and three months earlier, his family had buried his oldest brother John at the age of twenty-eight. It was right before Christmas, and the year was a celebration of firsts. It was John's four-month-old daughter's first Christmas, John's first as a father, and his parents and brothers' firsts as grandparents and uncles. While the time was emotional and trying for the whole family, Maher clearly remembers their spiritual maturity and their sense of gratitude, holding on to their faith that God is good. "That was the first time gratitude would become this foundation for my faith, and the second time was when the victim's son forgave me."

Maher was sentenced to serve five and a half years for aggravated manslaughter while driving under the influence. Most people would look at this situation and not see any good, but he saw the opposite—that God was sovereign, and He knew the exact decision Maher would make that would bring him to this precise place. Stripped of all he had held in his mind as his identity, fully humbled and now without any of his former self, Maher entered prison.

"I was so grateful to be forgiven and that my God is good, and that drove me the entire duration. I can honestly say that those fifty-five months felt like fifty-five days." He saw all around him the resentment and bitterness of the other inmates, living out the consequences for their own bad decisions. Maher, however, chose to see things through a different lens.

"God was giving me these case studies all around me, saying, 'Don't be shortsighted. Don't be blind. Be grateful. I have a plan.'" When looking back on the thoughts he had during that time, he wrote, "They are saturated in gratefulness."

He cites 1 Thessalonians 5:16 from the NIV that he constantly repeated: "Rejoice always, pray continuously, give thanks in all circumstances, for this is God's will for you in Christ Jesus."

While he was in prison, Maher and his brothers founded a publishing company called 5511 Publishing based on Isaiah

55:11, "So is my word that goes from my mouth: It will not return to me empty, but will accomplish what I desire and achieve the purpose for which I sent it." 5511 Publishing released Maher's first book, written while he was incarcerated.

Today, Matthew has shared his story to hundreds of thousands by speaking at events, churches, and schools. He continually tells his story of forgiveness, faith, and redemption. Upon his release from prison, he immediately resumed what he started while incarcerated—"Decisions Determine Destiny" assemblies. Through this program, he has reached over forty thousand high school and college students each year. Maher is also a pastor on staff at Coastal Christian Ocean City. He has a column, iCONVICTION, for the *Cape May County Herald*. He also contributes regularly to the online Christian movement website, EU Movement.

Maher speaks for the Be Still Foundation, a 501(c)(3) nonprofit ministry advocating responsible decision-making for the prevention of risky behaviors and prison ministry outreach. He has partnered in ministry with Debbie Kay's Hope for the Broken Hearted, and cohosts a Roku Channel TV show titled, *Surviving the Storm*.

Maher's story of being broken down to the bare bones and having his identity stripped away so suddenly is unimaginable. Few people would think of gratitude during this type of trial, but gratitude is exactly what Maher focused on as he lived through his incarceration and what turned a seemingly horrific, humiliating, life-tainting situation into a beautiful story of redemption.

While many of us won't endure such trials, we are guaranteed struggles and grief in our lifetime. If we can hold on to gratitude and remember how powerful it is to lift someone from down so low back into a full and prospering life, we too can take advantage of its power. Matthew just celebrated his daughter's first birthday and is living his most prosperous life now, fully grateful every day.

"The Lord forgives you, receives you, and is willing to use you in spite of you," he concluded.

"'For I know the plans I have for you,' declares the LORD, 'Plans to prosper you and not to harm you, plans to give you hope and a future.'"

JEREMIAH 29:11 NIV

How different would your life be if you took the prior verse to heart? Would the same anxieties and thoughts replay through your mind day after day? I believe it's important to repeat such verses to ourselves or write them down so they will be seen regularly. In my life, the times I was in the deepest despair didn't end up being the worst-case scenarios I envisioned, and the growth I experienced through my adversities was pivotal.

"Stand up straight and realize who you are, that you tower over your circumstances."

—MAYA ANGELOU

Both Sandberg and Maher grew exponentially from their experiences, and they now use their stories to help others. Many of us don't want to think about undesirable circumstances and try in every way to avoid or shelter others from them. Tiptoeing through life like this is like caging a sprout so it can't turn into a flower or preventing a chick from hatching. The most famous icons in history and the best movies are rich with tales of overcoming great adversity, and in each case, the most daunting trials stir the most emotion—turning into the best stories.

POWERFUL MOTIONS

But in bad times, the last thing we feel is gratitude! Arthur Brooks, former American Enterprise Institute president, spoke about the effectiveness of expressing thanks when we are not feeling grateful. When we do so, we may feel insincere or even fake.[41] Numerous studies that he cites, however, show the value of expressing gratitude regardless of how we feel.

"In a nutshell," he says, "acting grateful can actually make you grateful."[42]

Dr. Robert Emmons, a leading gratitude researcher, has more to say on this conundrum: "Under crisis conditions, we have the most to gain by a grateful perspective on life. In the face of demoralization, gratitude has the power to energize. In the face of brokenness, gratitude has the power to heal. In the face of despair, gratitude has the power to bring hope."

Emmons's research dives deep into the psychology of gratitude, along with the psychology of individual goal setting

---

41 Naz Beheshti. "Science Says You Shouldn't Wait for Things to Go Well Before Showing Gratitude."

42 Arthur C. Brooks. "Choose to Be Grateful. It Will Make You Happier."

and its correlation with positive outcomes. He has written six books, including *How the New Science of Gratitude Can Make You Happier,* and over a hundred articles.

Emmons advocates choosing a gratitude mind-set to help us make the best of all circumstances. He developed a strategy he calls "Remember the Bad." The point is to reflect on difficult times, remembering how we got past them so as not to dwell in a negative place. This practice reminds us what we have endured and gives us a way to express gratitude for how we got through it and to not take our blessings for granted.

To experience the full effects of gratitude is to maintain the practice in both good times and bad. This takes dedication and time, but with daily effort we will be able to switch over to the lens of gratitude. Once we can view all circumstances through the lens of gratitude, we will live our fullest lives regardless of what adversities arise.

The next time life doesn't go your way, try to keep this perspective in mind. Adversity through the lens of gratitude reveals miracle after miracle—one breath, day, and step at a time. It's very hard to do at first, but as it's practiced and refined, it gets easier and easier. Recall when you were learning how to do something impossibly difficult for the first time. Now remember when things clicked into place. Learning to ride a bike or playing a difficult piece of music are good examples. You develop the muscle memory and can hop on one at any time or play from memory without a second thought. This is similar. The more you practice gratitude, the quicker you will be able to catch your thoughts going to a dark place and shift your perspective back to all your blessings. God truly does have a plan for us. We just need to remember and hold on during the trials. Gratitude is a gift to see us through.

PUTTING IT INTO PRACTICE

Writing down three to five things you are grateful for when you first wake in the morning and right before you go to bed is one of the best ways to build this mind-set. I keep a notebook on my nightstand for this exact reason. If you get in the habit of doing this twice a day, you will be surprised how quickly your mind-set begins to change for the better. To expand on this exercise, think back to a tough time you went through and pull out all the good things that came of it.

CHAPTER 6

CONNECTION TO OTHERS

———

"Gratitude connects us to others, and feeling gratitude allows us to be our best selves. When we are truly grateful, we can count on living the life we want."

—M. J. RYAN

MIND-SET TO SUCCESS

When I think of connected people, some come to mind right away. The name Oprah is recognizable internationally, no last name needed. She is known for many things—talk show host, successful media magnate, philanthropist, billionaire, women's activist, and the list goes on.

Most people are aware that she came from humble beginnings. Oprah was born in 1954 in Mississippi. Soon after her birth, her parents separated, and her childhood was spent going back and forth between them. During these early years, Oprah experienced the lowest poverty, but she was also blessed to have key figures in her life to care for her and help grow her talents. Her grandmother helped her to read at three years of age, creating and fostering her love for books. She began with reading the Bible and would recite verses to her grandmother's friends. Upon entering kindergarten at five, she was quickly moved to first grade, since she could already read.

When she was six, she went to live with her mom in Milwaukee and was neglected, since her mom had to work long hours as a maid. When she was nine, she was raped by her nineteen-year-old cousin who was supposed to be caring for her. She suffered additional sexual abuse from her mother's boyfriend and other relatives before running away at age thirteen.

At fourteen, she became pregnant and seriously contemplated suicide. Before she could take action, she gave birth, and the baby died shortly after. Afterward, she went to Tennessee to live with her father, who called the loss "a second chance"— words she would remember throughout her life.

"I was, in many ways, saved by that, and I made a decision that I was going to turn it around," she said. Oprah credits her father's strict upbringing and his sound advice for shaping who she became, recalling how she had to recite new vocabulary nightly before she received dinner. She was active in her church and gave speeches and sermons. In her adolescence, she earned $500 for a speaking engagement. At that moment, she realized she wanted to speak to others as a career.[43]

Oprah's studies took her to Tennessee State University where, as only a nineteen-year-old sophomore, she was offered her first job as a co-anchor for CBS Nashville. She was on the fast track from there, moving on to Baltimore, then Chicago where she was given her first opportunity to connect to an audience in a talk show format. Her ratings were so high, it forced Phil Donahue, who previously had the highest-rated talk show in Chicago, to move his show to New York. *The Oprah Winfrey Show* took hold, and the rest is history.

Oprah's connection to others is obvious when watching her interview and host guests. She is respectfully curious, always open to learn and be enlightened. She is emotionally connected and shows her vulnerability without trying to hide it or ever pretending to be something she is not. In the years of her award-winning talk show, she often shared with

---

43   Elizabeth Fry. "Did Oprah's Childhood Shape Her Career?"

the audience and guests her own struggles, especially with weight. Being so authentic and relatable, she quickly gained the trust of others, and the stories shared were emotional, uplifting, motivational, and, above all, memorable.

She remained grounded, and although her fortunes grew immense, few judge her for her wealth, but instead respect her for what she has accomplished.

"The human experience of yours is stunning," David Letterman said to Oprah during an interview at Ball State University.

"I am so grateful for my years literally living in poverty," she replied, "because it makes the experience of creating success and building success that much more rewarding."

Time and time again, Oprah has credited her daily practice of gratitude for her success and fulfillment. "The more thankful I became, the more my bounty increased. That's because—for sure—what you focus on expands. When you focus on the goodness in life, you create more of it." When she would have guests on her show, she would so deeply feel her gratitude and privilege that it would often transfer to her guests as well.

One particular guest she had on her show, Monica Jorge, had gone into the hospital for a routine delivery of her second child. During her brief stay, she contracted a vicious flesh-eating bacteria. To save her life, she had to have both arms and both legs amputated. In her interview with Oprah, she says her consuming thought during her ordeal was that she needed to get home to take care of her kids.

Later Oprah recalls in her book, *What I Know for Sure*, how she went to reach for something and was overcome with gratitude that she had arms to reach for it. "The only prayer that is ever needed is "thank you." Nothing is guaranteed, and we need to deeply feel all that we do have and realize the good in every situation," said Oprah.

While Oprah kept a gratitude journal for years by her bed, she admits that there was a period when she was building the Oprah Winfrey Network (OWN) that she got away from the practice, and as a result, she felt much less fulfillment and joy from that experience.

"Being grateful all the time isn't easy. But it's when you feel the least thankful that you are in most need of what gratitude can give you—perspective," she recounts. "I'm still trying to wrap my head around the idea that the girl from Mississippi who grew up holding her nose in an outhouse now flies on her own plane—my own plane!—to Africa to help girls who grew up like her."

Perspective is the gift that gratitude offers, and if you are able to change your mind-set to reflect that, you will be overwhelmed at the transformation that takes place. When I first began to study gratitude, the very first quote that struck me was from Oprah: "Be thankful for what you have. You'll end up having more. If you concentrate on what you don't have, you will never ever have enough."

If Oprah can come from the lowest level of poverty with a perspective of gratitude, anyone can, starting here and now. The lens of gratitude can be a monumental mental shift in anyone's life. This perspective (and her authenticity) is what immediately draws others to her, and the connection she cultivates is powerful. Her story could span most other chapters in this book as well, because she exemplifies a life of gratitude to the fullest extent and, consequently, reaps the benefits. We will circle back to Oprah again in Chapter 8.

CONNECTION VERSUS COMPARISON—A SLIPPERY SLOPE

When we first meet people, it's natural for us to make some mental comparisons, but those comparisons can head down a negative path if we are not careful.

Frans de Waal and his colleagues at the Yerkes National Primate Research Center in Atlanta, Georgia decided to try several primate experiments with thirteen capuchin monkeys to retrieve a rock and give it to the experimenter for a "payout" reward. Pairs of monkeys were seated next to each other in test booths separated by mesh so they could see what was happening with their neighbor.[44]

The monkeys were asked to give a pebble and were both happy to receive a piece of cucumber as a reward. Interestingly enough, when they were asked to do the same task and given different rewards, the outcome changed. One monkey was given the cucumber, but another a grape. Monkeys highly regard grapes, and the one given the cucumber was upset with this comparison and threw the cucumber back at the instructor.

---

44   Megan Van Wolkenten , Sarah F. Brosnan, and Frans BM de Waal. "Inequity Responses of Monkeys Modified by Effort." (18854)

Through this primate experiment, I see such a correlation between the downside of social media and the inevitable comparison that often happens in our minds. For adults, it's sometimes hard to see a friend or coworker off on a tropical vacation, getting recognized in some situation, or enjoying a success when we ourselves aren't having the best day. Dr. Tracy Brower, a sociologist who has researched and written articles on the topic, says, "Social media can be terrible for your health. It makes you feel connected (when you're not), and it can contribute to depression and unfavorable comparisons."[45]

For children, this hits even deeper because their brains are still developing. If they use social media and see friends invited to something they weren't, a comparison can happen in their minds, and this contributes to FOMO, as we discussed in Chapter 3.[46] Comparison is inevitable, but with social media, it's in your face twenty-four seven without escape. For children who are more likely to compare when seeing a visual of reality, it's especially concerning.

Twenty years ago, if a party happened and I didn't know about it, I was happy in my blissful ignorance. But today, if I see images of that party—say with all my neighbors, and I wasn't invited—it stings, if only for a minute, but that comparison happens, nonetheless. According to Joseph Reagle, "Fear of missing out results from the new and increasing addiction to social media."

---

45   Tracy Brower. "Yes, Social Media Is Making You Miserable."

46   Vittoria Franchina, et al. "Fear of Missing Out as a Predictor of Problematic Social Media Use and Phubbing Behavior Among Flemish Adolescents." (2319)

Subconsciously, what goes on in your mind from that point on is arguable, as a lot depends on many other factors. It does seem, however, to have an impact beyond that initial feeling of being left out. I also believe it's exponentially problematic in youth still trying to negotiate the social hierarchy that has always been one of the most challenging aspects of middle school to college-aged kids.

"A heart at peace gives life to the body, but envy rots the bones."
PROVERBS 14:30 NIV

GRATITUDE AND CONNECTION THROUGH LOSS

Kelly grew up in Newfoundland, Canada, an island with a total population of around five hundred thousand. Life in this rugged, rural, remote, and often harsh climate was sometimes rough. She describes her childhood self as a sunny-side up personality, often finding joy in the little things to get through the bad. She left Canada for North Carolina and enjoyed working as a nurse and raising her two boys alongside her husband.

She and her husband were out of state the night she got the call that would forever change her life.

"There has been an accident."

Kelly and her husband rushed to Jordan Lake in North Carolina where her son Stephen and his friends had been boating and swimming that Fourth of July holiday.

"He was an invincible kid," she remembers, "so athletic and capable, you would never think anything could happen to him during any physical play like swimming."

What they later found out was that Stephen had been hit in the chest by a hockey puck, and although he seemed fine, a blood clot had formed at the site of the injury.

They drove through the night and got to the lake near dawn. Upon arriving and seeing the divers, she felt gutted.

"I've always been able to figure out a plan B quickly," she told me, "but I felt like I was tapping around looking for the rug, but along with the rug, the entire floor was taken out from beneath me." She didn't know what she was going to do or how she was going to get through this.

The divers found Stephen's body that day, and it was determined that the blood clot from the puck trauma had moved to his lung while he was swimming, causing him to drown. Stephen was a twin whose brother had died at birth.

"I never properly grieved Matthew," she said. "I tucked the pain away and tried to move on. When Stephen died, I finally embraced the pain of also losing Matthew."

Looking back now, she realizes the clarity she got that morning as she wrote little things she was grateful for on the back of her cable bill while she sat in her car at the funeral home. This would later evolve into her book *Gratitude in Grief.*

She was thankful for the divers, and that they found his body. She realized in that moment how many parents don't get the closure of seeing their child's body after they have passed. All of Stephen's friends and their parents were so available and consoling to Kelly and her family. She remembers one mom hugging her and the gratitude she felt.

"This woman hugged me just like my mom, who passed away in 1991, so it was like my mom sending me a hug from heaven."

Kelly's story of tragedy has morphed into a platform to help others. From her book has stemmed her blog, and from there, her Facebook group, Just One Little Thing, which has over 130,000 followers. The subtitle to her group is "A Global Community of Resilience and Gratitude."

"Happiness is found moment by moment, and always in the little things," says Kelly. Her surviving son, at just twelve years old, made her promise to respond to everyone who reached out to her. "Because if they reach out to you, it means they are hurting like we are," he said. She has done just that and continues to do so every day.

After countless prayers, Kelly heard a whisper from God. He spoke directly to Kelly during her darkest hour of grief, when she was a broken mom who lost her son without any warning. She recalls trying to negotiate with God before listening to him. He led her to gratitude to get her through loss, and in practicing gratitude, she and her family have never been closer.

The community she has built will forever be grateful to Kelly for her beacon of hope and happiness after tragedy hit. Connection to others through gratitude and the realization that we are not alone can heal even the deepest wounds. I'm amazed by what God can do through people when they let him, and I wonder, how often is he whispering to us when we let other things drown him out?

"The LORD said, 'Go out and stand on the mountain in the presence of the LORD, for the LORD is about to pass by.' Then a great and powerful wind tore the mountains apart and shattered the rocks before the LORD, but the LORD was not in the wind. After the wind there was an earthquake, but the LORD was not in the earthquake. After the earthquake came a fire, but the LORD was not in the fire. And after the fire came a gentle whisper."

1 KINGS 19:11–12 NIV

GRATITUDE CAN BE THE GREATEST GIFT WE GIVE

Andrew Horn struggled with social anxiety and shyness his whole life. He tells of times he got stuck in his head, concerned about what others were thinking about him, which reinforced the vicious cycle. He worked hard on his issues, focusing on being extremely curious about people to get past his anxiety.

"If we're worried about what people think of us, we aren't present. If we're not present, we can't be ourselves, and we won't fully connect," Andrew states.

Looking inward and working on his own insecurities gave him the confidence to go after something that was important to him. After college, he went on to found a nonprofit that connected kids to elite athletes, which brought him success. One day, when his girlfriend gave him an unexpected gift, he first experienced gratitude in a way that would shape his life and career.

He describes a low-key birthday party with several friends and colleagues gathered at his apartment to hang out. Around the time when things might start to wrap up, his girlfriend asked everyone to gather in the back room. It didn't seem that odd—perhaps he had a cake or a gift to open. As everyone settled, a video began to play. On it, Andrew's friends and family expressed why he was so important to them and what he meant to them in words and emotion. His mother recounts, "You are wealthy in what matters…and I'm so appreciative of it."

Talking about this special moment, Andrew's enthusiasm really starts to come through. "When I got to sit in the back of the room and watch twenty of my friends and family members tell me why they loved and respect me…I really felt this deep, foundational sense of self-worth and self-love."

What an interesting perspective on gratitude from someone who struggled with interpersonal connection.

"As someone who's dealt with social anxiety my whole life, I always had this constant internal critic, this imposter syndrome in so many situations," he explains. "And I think so many people can relate with that. To hear the people who I respected and cared about telling me why they love me, that part of the brain that was always so critical just shut up…it just led me to accept this." And it said, 'If you matter in the lives of these people who matter most to you, you're good.'"

So powerful and true. How could this world change if everyone got to hear such accolades from those closest to them at this young age, or any age, for that matter?

"I took that confidence, that connection, with me every single day," Andrew says. "It allowed me to be a little kinder to myself, to be a little more confident, grateful—a little happier. And when I understood the power, that was ultimately what really showed me that this was not just a gift."

Not just a gift, but something much bigger that could help others. Andrew experienced life-changing gratitude for this amazing gift. His girlfriend had spent countless hours putting it together, truly a monumental effort. But what if he could streamline this process so that others could experience what he had without so much work? Not long after his birthday celebration, Tribute.co was born—a company centered around expressing gratitude and helping others recreate what he himself had experienced.

Today, over a quarter million tributes have been created and shared, gratitude has been expressed, and lives have been altered.

"I'm really passionate about giving as many people on earth that experience of being totally and fully seen by the people that they care about. Because I think that ultimately, when people experience being fully seen, recognized, and appreciated, they want to pay that forward...because the feeling is undeniable. It's this embodied kind of recognition that you're valued. And when we feel that, we want to also express that to who matters most to us."

Andrew has a powerful testimony on the transformative effects of gratitude. He reminded me of a common saying we often hear as kids. "If you don't have anything nice to say, don't say anything at all." Andrew shifted a few words around to make a much more powerful statement: "If you have anything nice to say, say it all."

That perfectly wraps up his company, Tribute.co, but it's also a powerful reminder to live fully while expressing our appreciation to others. You often hear sad stories where a loved one passes unexpectedly and those left behind wish their last conversation with that person was more meaningful. Living life with this in mind would reduce those types of regrets.

Andrew summarizes, "I really believe that if one of your objectives is to be happy, but you do not have time for gratitude every day, then you simply don't have time to be happy. It's so easy—it takes sixty seconds, and it's scientifically proven."

What really strikes me about Andrew's story is how quickly gratitude connects people. Technology and social media are ironically disconnecting us from others, but gratitude brings us so much closer together. In my life, social media has been the negative comparison that I didn't anticipate, just like the monkeys comparing their reward to their neighbor's.

Gratitude not only counteracts that comparison but shows us what we have in common with our neighbors.

"So in everything, do to others what you would have them do to you, for this sums up the Law and the Prophets."

MATTHEW 7:12 NIV

Dr. Robert Emmons of the Greater Good Science Center has provided the research to back this up. People who practice gratitude acknowledge the help of others and prioritize their time with those who matter most. "Gratitude really helps us connect to other people," Emmons says. "It actually strengthens relationships, and relationships are the strongest predictors of happiness and coping with stress."[47]

PUTTING IT INTO PRACTICE

Facilitating connection through gratitude is one of the easiest practices to implement and reap the fastest rewards. Most of us can bring to mind someone we love unconditionally. Taking five minutes to dwell on this person and the feelings and memories that you've built with them is a great starting point. Along with these feelings, rehearse in your mind all the reasons you feel grateful for that person. Then project that by thinking of people you are looking to further connect with and feel gratitude for that connection. Doing this exercise regularly will strengthen the connection you have beyond your expectations. Chapter 9 will go much more in depth in practicing gratitude.

---

47   Lindsay Holmes. "10 Things Grateful People Do Differently."

"Above all, love each other deeply, because love covers over a multitude of sins."

1 PETER 4:8 NIV

CHAPTER 7

TRUE HAPPINESS

———

"Happiness cannot be traveled to, owned, earned, worn, or consumed. Happiness is the spiritual experience of living every minute with love, grace, and gratitude."

—DENIS WAITLEY

VIEW THROUGH A CLEAR LENS

When observing the life of the Dalai Lama, one thing strikes me more than any other: he laughs…a lot. In interviews, videos, photos, and with others, he has found joy, and it's overflowing from him often. Sometimes the mood is somber and serious, then he will crack a joke and bring laughter to everyone else in the room, delivering joy to those around him—what a gift to share! He is truly happy and has shared his wisdom for finding this place of joy and happiness within ourselves, right where we are now. But what is his secret?

"The roots of all goodness lie in the soil of appreciation for goodness."

—THE DALAI LAMA

The Dalai Lama always comes from a place of warmhearted kindness, which greatly reduces negative feelings between others. He connects easily to people. They don't have their guard up and therefore are not distrustful. Additionally, he never considers himself anything special.

"If I consider myself any different from you…then you create yourself as a prisoner."

He thinks of himself as intellectually, emotionally, and physically the same as the other seven billion humans on the earth.

Taking ego out of the mind opens us up to fully connect with others on the same level.

He stresses that we have within us the full potential to be completely happy. If we choose to do something negative to one another, we receive that back upon ourselves. Conversely, if we choose to do something that helps someone else or makes them happy, we get that back. He explains that when we are young, we innately know this and live this way. However, as we grow and see the world around us, we get pulled away into a material, selfish, "what's best for us" mentality. We don't advertise or promote warm-heartedness.[48]

We are taught from a young age to fear everything and everyone, which, he states, is a direct deterrent to friendship, a necessity to happiness. With fear, we cannot build trust, and without trust, we cannot build friendships. Loneliness has become an epidemic and the number one cause of depression in the western world. One in five Americans feel lonely or socially isolated, and two in five declare their social relationships are not meaningful either sometimes or always. Researchers have found that loneliness and social isolation can be as damaging to one's health as smoking fifteen cigarettes a day.[49]

The Dalai Lama paints the picture of a massive city with people everywhere, in all directions, passing each other in close proximity. I see the streets of New York City near Times Square. The mentality of self-centeredness isolates so many

---

48   "Questions & Answers." The 14th Dalai Lama.
49   Health Resources & Services Administration. "The 'Loneliness Epidemic.'"

in a prison within themselves, floating like a raft lost out at sea. This coupled with a lack of self-love, excess competition, and jealousy brings about distrust that in turn brings frustration, fear, then finally—loneliness. This imagery shows that someone in a sea of people can inwardly feel so alone.

With this realization, we can understand how we became unhappy, and therefore we can choose to change and become happy. Not only are a lot of bad things in the world around us, but a lot of good things are as well, and we need to keep our focus on all the good.

Gratitude and the perspective it brings comes into play here. The Dalai Lama encourages everyone to think each morning, "Today I am fortunate to be alive. I have a precious human life. I am not going to waste it. I am going to use all my energies to develop myself, to expand my heart out to others, to achieve enlightenment for the benefit of all beings. I am going to have kind thoughts toward others. I am not going to get angry or think badly about others. I am going to benefit others as much as I can."

His perspective must be a focal point—we always have something to be grateful for, and all other good will flow from that place of gratitude. "I find hope in the darkest of days and focus on the brightest," he says.

With such a strong focus on others, his story could have also appeared in Chapter 6. Gratitude, however, ties everything together. It will become apparent—if it hasn't already—that every story will have multiple aspects of gratitude. I hope you are seeing the commonality in all the stories thus far.

"When you are discontent, you always want more, more, more. Your desire can never be satisfied. But when you practice contentment, you can say to yourself, 'Oh yes—I already have everything that I really need.'" The Dalai Lama goes on to say that we already have enough, and if we choose to see that, we can be happy. "We don't need more money. We don't need greater success or fame. We don't need the perfect body or even the perfect mate. Right now, at this very moment, we have a mind, which is all the basic equipment we need to achieve complete happiness." He exemplifies gratitude.

Pessimism grows from a lost sense of hope or optimism. Roots set in gratitude will grow happiness.

The Dalai Lama has, in a very effective way, summed up the secret to happiness, and it lies within us right now in our current circumstances—if we choose to look inwardly and be grateful for all we have and are and view others in the same light. He is a real beacon that radiates a message of true contentment. We can learn from him that we don't need anything else in our lives to enjoy happiness every day, we just need to open our eyes to all the splendor we already have around us. From that vantage point, we see the good in others, and judgment and distrust melt away—we are as children again.

"There are two ways to live your life. One is as though nothing is a miracle. The other is as though everything is a miracle."
—ALBERT EINSTEIN

BEYOND TRIBULATION

I met Monique not long ago through a friend. Her warm smile and matching hug were infectious. My first impression of her was spot on. She had a big, glowing smile, and we instantly hit it off. As we chatted, she brought up the many things she was grateful for, and it was obvious she was living in a mind-set of gratitude. We discussed how things were different in the United States from where she grew up in Rwanda.

She mentioned how she was trying to instill things like gratitude in all situations in her daughter, who recently found out she was pregnant.[50] "In my home country, at that time, being pregnant as an unwed girl was a sacrilege." Girls were shamed for being pregnant out of wedlock. Pregnancy and childbirth in Rwanda had "no celebration because nothing is guaranteed."

While some similarities exist in Western culture depending on a pregnancy's parental circumstances, what strikes me most is how soon news is shared in the United States. We announce pregnancies so early, have baby showers and gender reveal parties. Americans celebrate and anticipate because we enjoy nearly 100 percent certainty of the baby's survival. In Rwandan culture at that time, they didn't celebrate until the baby was eight days old.

"Nobody sees the mother or baby until that time, unless you are a very close family member, and no one would even hold the baby," she tells me. "On the eighth day was the naming

---

50   Since the time of our interview, she has given birth to a baby boy.

ceremony that included giving thanks and offering to God in celebration."

In countries like Rwanda, the infant mortality rate is still considerably high, and everyone knows this, and therefore nothing is taken for granted or celebrated prematurely. Monique was the youngest of twelve children in her family, but her mother, along with many other women there, experienced miscarriages and losses prior to Monique's birth.

She described to me her close-knit community where everyone was involved in raising the children and helping each other out. Discipline was doled out when appropriate, and she tells a story of a time she made a mistake and was reprimanded by her neighbor and again by her mother when she got back home. Wisdom was also passed on through the community by the elders, who were respected in their culture. When someone needed something, people stepped in to help, and everyone was content.

From 1990 to 1994, however, political and military unrest reigned in the country. Tension was simmering, but Monique still felt that things were under control and safe. In hindsight, however, she recognized signs that things were going astray. People would suddenly disappear. Healthy people would die mysteriously, but it was never enough to send an alarm throughout the community. Unbeknownst to most of the people, arms were also being stockpiled and hidden throughout the country during these years of unrest.

On April 7, 1994, everything changed in an instant when a plane carrying the president of Rwanda and his entire cabinet crashed, leaving no survivors. The killing spree immediately began, during which time Monique's husband was killed while protecting their children. Nobody felt safe, teenagers and youth as young as nine were drugged, given weapons, and used to slaughter innocent people. The casualties included children, friends, and neighbors; killing was random and unrelenting. In this unimaginable chaos, Monique, who was twenty-eight at the time, summoned all her strength as a mother to fight to protect her then nine, six, and eighteen-month-old children.

She alludes to the silent pain, agony, shame, fear, and distress. The toxic grief and the psychological trauma that would ensue will be etched in her memory for the rest of her life, as it is for many Rwandans to this day. The constant battle for survival was grueling. She describes having to jump over corpses and mutilated bodies in the street, assaulted from every angle, terrified as she ran from one hiding spot to another. Things we see in movies or video games were *happening* to her.

The shouts and screams still haunt her to this day. Their voices play like recordings in her mind.

"We will kill you and your kids too!"

"Please help me."

Monique was trapped in the country her family called home, each day not knowing who was going to make it through the night. To call that a challenge would be an understatement; it was unrelenting horror.

For Monique, the dawn of a new day was a miracle, and it filled her with a deep sense of gratitude. Even though they may not have eaten or known the next time they would have food, they were all alive and, for the moment, together and safe. She continued to describe the most desolate of conditions—no food, dirty water if any, constant fear for her life and those of her children—yet she felt gratitude amid all the pain and suffering.

When I try to imagine even a sliver of what she was experiencing, tears well in my eyes. As a mother of three, I can't imagine the fear of the unknown in that situation or how I would press through. Would I have felt gratitude in that moment? Absolutely not.

After a long four-month journey on foot, God provided Monique and her children passage across the border into Burundi, and then on to Ghana. There they would spend the next eight years alone and in desperate need, but alive, together, and safe at last.

"It took years for me to trust people again."

Monique admits her deepest fear at that time was that her children would fall into despair, and she needed to do anything she could to ensure that wouldn't happen.

Each day in Ghana, she would watch a TV show called *The Living Word*, and she felt compelled to go meet the pastor who preached to her in her home. Upon entering the church, the staff tried to prevent her from meeting with him, but he happened to come out, and she went right up to him and told him her story, not knowing what to expect next.

"Monique, your life will never be the same again," he said, and from that day on, he made good on his promise.

She didn't have access to transportation, so the church set up a means for her family to get to and from the church regularly. They checked in on Monique's family and brought them food, brought the kids into the church for teaching and fellowship, and helped all her kids get into school. Although she was embraced, they never forced any religion on Monique or asked her for anything in return. This experience had a lasting impact on Monique.

The fear she had for the future of her children was unrelenting, and even though she felt safe and taken care of, she knew she would have this fear as long as they remained in Africa. She made the heart-wrenching decision to send her kids to France with family while she went to the United States.

She flew through Dulles International Airport outside of Washington, DC, before continuing to Alabama where she was immediately embraced by a community of caring people who quickly became her friends. Her stay there was brief, and she soon found herself in Richmond, Virginia, with a job as a medical claims adjuster while she attended a local community college. She became an advocate for seniors and helped them get their medical bills paid, but she knew she wasn't where she was supposed to be. Through prayer and consideration, she got her answer: "Come back to where you first landed." To her, this meant Dulles Airport in Loudoun County, Virginia.

Monique left her job and studies and followed her message from God. She was immediately connected to more friends, ultimately finding a job caring for the elderly just a few miles from the airport. Monique has a special relationship with the aging community and helps them connect with family, especially during their last days. She tells me a heartwarming story of an elderly woman who knew it was her time, and she wanted to see her daughter one last time to celebrate. They did just that—a full celebration with cake, balloons, and much laughter and tears. Shortly after, the woman passed, and Monique gets a postcard every year from the woman's daughter, telling her it was the best gift she has ever gotten, and she is eternally grateful.

With a sigh, Monique told me, "You cannot ask 'why me' but must be grateful for everything at all times, for everything we go through is for a purpose." She put her arms around herself as if in an embrace, closed her eyes, and seemed to meditate on the next phrase as she spoke. "I say thank you that my kids were saved, thank you for sharing my story, thank you for allowing me to speak to others in this way to help them through their most difficult times."

My time with her and her powerful story will forever be etched in my memory, along with the reminder to be grateful in every situation.

"When we can say thank you for the smallest things, the ones that we take for granted, that is the most powerful thing," she declared.

Monique is truly content today and finds fulfillment in her relationship with God and her work with elders. Having gone through it all, she has radically accepted her experiences as a testament to God's goodness and the gift of gratitude he has given to us. For me, Monique's example is a reminder that we can also find contentment and happiness regardless of our past or current circumstances.

"Why would God allow such things to happen?" is a question I have heard many times in my life. When we dissect our circumstances and pull out the bad parts, we tend to ask such things. But when we have faith and use the gift of gratitude, we can shift our perspectives and find the good, no matter how small. We are also then able to see the overwhelming good in the continuum of our lives, even in the negative events we must face to grow and make us stronger.

"You have turned my mourning into joyful dancing. You have taken away my clothes of mourning and clothed me with joy."
PSALM 30:11 NLT

RECIPE FOR OPTIMISM

Dr. Robert Emmons teamed up with Dr. Michael McCullough of the University of Miami for another study on gratitude. In this study, they asked all participants to focus on specific topics they were given and write a few sentences each week.

One group was asked to write about things they were grateful for that had happened over the week. A second group wrote about the aggravations or negative things that had affected them that past week, and the third was asked to write about the events of their week without positive or negative connotations. After ten weeks, those who wrote about gratitude reported being more optimistic about their circumstances and their lives. Surprisingly, they also reported to have exercised more and required fewer doctor visits than people in the other two groups. No notable changes in positive outlook were reported in the other two groups.[51] This study is in line with what we have been seeing on a consistent basis with the practice of gratitude. It would have been interesting if they had reported back on a weekly basis how long it took the benefits of gratitude to take effect. In my own experience, it happened very quickly.

Implementing practices of gratitude that lead to true happiness begins with experiencing the feeling on a daily basis. As in the study above, this takes some time, but if kept up with, it can have a positive, long-lasting impact on your life. In this chapter, we saw two individuals who exuded true happiness. Both endured hardships and chose to view life through the lens of gratitude, contributing to the happiness they live day to day.

PUTTING IT INTO PRACTICE

Try keeping colorful sticky notes around in places you might have a free moment, like your bathroom sink, car, or in the kitchen. Use the colorful reminders to jot down things you

---

51   Harvard Health Publishing. "Giving Thanks Can Make You Happier."

are grateful for and post them where you will see them. This activity builds upon itself, as the more you do it, the more you will remember to live gratefully. You can also use the Growing Gratitude Tree[52] to build a beautiful visual reminder of all you have in your life.

---

52 Available at www.gratitudemission.org.

CHAPTER 8

ABUNDANCE

―

*"When you are grateful, fear disappears,
and abundance appears."*

—TONY ROBBINS

STOP SEARCHING AND OPEN YOUR EYES

So far, we've explored gratitude's therapeutic properties—healing and getting one's life back on a positive trajectory. Eckhart Tolle, a spiritual teacher and an author of many books, including *The Power of Now*, has a lot more to say on the topic of gratitude. The way he perceives gratitude takes things to a whole other level of incredible abundance, as you are about to find out. He tells the story of a beggar sitting on a street with nothing, asking for the kindness of strangers passing by. One stranger approaches him and says he has nothing to offer him but can help the beggar if he has something to give to the stranger in return.

The beggar is perplexed and tells the stranger he has nothing to give.

"What about the box you are sitting on? I have been searching for such a box," the stranger tells him.

Still confused, the beggar gets up and with the help of the stranger lifts the cover off the filthy, small box he was sitting on, surprised to find it full of gold. Eckhart uses this story to illustrate that what people search for externally—fulfillment, joy, happiness, peace, security, love, and validation, to name a few—is illusive. He argues that all the treasure we seek, even infinitely greater, is already within us, just waiting to be discovered and enjoyed.

This wasn't always his mind-set. In fact, Tolle was just shy of his twenty-ninth birthday and had lived his life up until that point in "continuous anxiety interspersed with depression." He remembered beginning the day with a deep loathing of the world and a greater longing for the end of life rather than life itself. He became aware of this strange and peculiar thought, sensing that he had only one perspective of himself and that there must be another self as well.

Then he entered a deep, trancelike sleep, and the last thing he recalls is terror and feeling drawn into a vortex of energy, hearing only the words "resist nothing" as if he was being sucked into a void. At that point, he let go, noticing his fear disappear at that same moment.

Tolle awoke to the chirping of a bird. He had never heard such a sound before and felt as if he was hearing for the first time. "If a diamond could make a sound, this is what it is," he recalled thinking. A soft light was the second thing he remembered, coming through as love, or at least that is how it felt to him.

Everything he experienced was fresh and pristine, as if he had just been born. The next five months, he lived in a state of uninterrupted peace and bliss that afterward diminished only slightly in intensity. He went searching for what he had experienced, reading many spiritual texts and meeting with spiritual leaders to finally realize that what he had experienced was what everyone is looking for—to live fully in the present moment, to have an "awakening," so to speak.

"When you are open to the present moment, what comes in is gratitude for what is, good in everything, and peace," Tolle explains.[53]

He takes the power of gratitude beyond this though, stating, "Acknowledging the good that you already have in your life is the foundation for all abundance." When you go deeply into the present, gratitude arises spontaneously, even if it's just gratitude for breathing, gratitude for the life that you feel in your body. Gratitude is not just a means to fulfillment, joy, and happiness, but "the foundation for all abundance." Tolle goes deeper into how and why.

First we must address the negative emotions and states in our lives. For instance, if we try to be aware of the "energy" of anger, fear, resentment, or pessimism and recognize it as an expression of held pain, we must stay aware of these thoughts as a witness to them in the present situation. By detaching from our self, we see as another would looking into our situation, and this disconnects us (or our identity) from the negative emotion. This awareness is the real catalyst to change from "being angry" to "observing angry."

"In the first few seconds," Tolle instructs, "be thankful for the anger, for growing awareness and spiritual growth. Recognize the thought forms are not truth when they are negative."

He describes that every movie always has something go wrong, and a character grows from that event, and we should

53   Clarified Pickle. "Eckhart Tolle & His Enlightenment—How It Happened."

look at our lives in this way and be thankful for everything, even difficulties as they create awareness and growth.

"All stress comes from resisting the present moment," Tolle says. "The primary cause of unhappiness is never the situation but your thoughts about it."

Many wealthy people are unhappy, still deprived of the fullness of life, especially when their wealth comes from a need to prove something to the world. From deep dissatisfaction, they accumulate more and more, yet it is never enough to quench this inner thirst. Tolle says, "When we have an eye on the goal or future as a means to an end…it will always reduce the present moment." This future focus looks past the present as not enough. "Believing that something in the future will bring you fulfillment is a lie. If you don't have it now, you won't have it then."

Rich means to be in touch with the fullness of life, love, and the present moment through the lens of gratitude. This is the foundation of wealth and intense *aliveness*, he argues, to feel that fullness of life within. He goes further to say that to know what you're doing to help others also brings wealth. Therefore, external wealth is a manifestation of an inner reality, cultivated and brought forth through gratitude. In a discussion with Oprah about his book *A New World*, Tolle claims letting in gratitude changes your vibrational frequency so much that "if you only remember one thing from this book, bring gratitude into your life."[54]

---

54 Peacefulness "Eckhart Tolle and Oprah Winfrey—Abundance and Gratitude."

The abundance from gratitude is like a geyser gushing up from the ground—it was in us the whole time and is now being released. Additionally, the spiritual connection becomes abundant to all who have found gratitude. And as Tolle describes above, gratitude leads to a desire to help others, which brings even more fulfillment into our lives.

HIGHER AND HIGHER

Krista Woods was a mom with three kids, a hectic life, and not much extra time. Her son was playing lacrosse, and the moms would take turns carpooling to and from practice and games. As with any sport, a lot of gear had to be transported along with the players, and lacrosse was no exception. Over time, Woods' minivan would get a pervasive wet-gear smell that would not dissipate. On one of those after-game runs, she told her husband she would need to find a solution.

The various things on the market didn't help her problem at all and were filled with awful chemicals. She realized a need for a better solution. Woods decided to invent one and created GloveStix to address the situation. Her husband came up with the first prototype in their garage using PVC pipes. After much trial and error, they came up with something that worked, then shopped around to assess the need, and after some time, Woods had a winning solution.

She and her family started with what they knew—lacrosse—and began selling out of a tent at her son's tournaments. Each time, they would sell out and invest what they earned to do it again on a bigger scale. She describes the ups and downs of "out of your trunk" sales, like the time they all drove fifteen hours to Florida for a tournament that ended up being rained out. "Life is like a wheel. Sometimes you're on top and sometimes on the bottom," Woods says.

Having started my own business, I can attest to this feeling; you are constantly taking one step forward, one step back. I would second-guess myself, then, after a mistake, come down hard on my decision—even though my product was about gratitude and I was practicing it regularly! Old mental patterns can be so hard to break and will creep in at opportune times to derail the good.

"I never would have dreamed the last three years would have turned out like this," says Woods. She describes herself as confident but resistant to the spotlight. An opportunity came up to apply for *The Today Show's* "Next Big Thing" invention *momtrepreneur* competition, which she entered. Weeks later, she was on air as a finalist and ended up winning. The next day, she appeared on QVC and sold out her inventory in seven and a half minutes. "When we got back after that amazing few days, reality set in, and now I had to ship and fulfill thousands of units in a certain time frame."

Woods describes the chaos at her home where family, friends, and friends of friends all showed up to help out for some free pizza. "The only thing I look back and think about is gratitude. I'm so grateful to my family, my friends, my kids' friends...and to God because despite thinking and feeling like it many times, I didn't quit, and that experience will be one of the most incredible of my lifetime."

Business continued to grow, and Woods had the opportunity to apply to be on *Shark Tank*. Woods recounts being completely transparent during the numerous interview rounds, as she wanted to share the truth about all the adversities she had overcome. However, when she found out she was going to be sent to filming, the psychological warfare began. Would the sharks know about all her failures, mistakes, and vulnerabilities that she had divulged in the interview rounds? What would she be made to look like on national television? This continued feeling of worry and anxiety led to sleepless nights, and for six months, she experienced so much unnecessary stress.

At one point during filming, an onslaught began, and she teared up but pulled herself back together. Woods walked out of *Shark Tank* with a huge smile and a verbal deal from Lori Greiner and Alex Rodriguez. All those months of worry and anxiety—for what? Even though the deal fell through as terms were changed, in the end, she admits it was all worth it, as GloveStix sold an entire year's inventory in only two months after the episode aired, and her business continues to grow year after year. Woods recalls that during the process, she let worry and fear about the unknown get the best of her at times. She admits she forgot to "simply be grateful for what I was doing and learning. Gratitude is a continual practice, and I am constantly reminded to check my mind-set to make sure I don't fall back to old habits."

I could feel Woods' passion coming through as she exclaimed, "If you compare yourself to others, you will always find someone smarter or better at something than you. Never compare yourself—use your energy to look inside and find your greatness."

This resonates with me at the core. We all have so much God-given talent, and we only need to look within and be grateful, then we can watch the magic unfold.

"And my God will meet all your needs according to the riches of his glory in Christ Jesus."

PHILIPPIANS 4:19 NIV

The abundance I have seen come into my life since I started to embrace gratitude is nothing short of miraculous. I can't look back and argue that it was luck, timing, or my perseverance in any of the situations that have come my way the past few years. I went on a journey to understand the roots of happiness and found gratitude and, through it, a transformation of my life. My journey didn't start with a step but a rocket booster into the life and happiness I now get to wake up to every day—feeling fulfilled, excited, and curious for what will come next.

Let us circle back to Oprah again. She credits her abundance to the gratitude she expresses. Others who share her same observation, such as Wayne Dyer, Eckhart Tolle, and Jack Canfield, have similarly accrued much wealth and prominence.

GRATITUDE FOR WHAT'S TO COME

Dr. Joe Dispenza has a theory:

Gratitude is a powerful emotion to use for manifesting the future because normally we feel gratitude after we receive something. So the emotional signature of gratitude means it has already happened. When you are thankful or you feel appreciation, you are in the ultimate state to receive. When you embrace gratitude, your body as the unconscious mind will begin to believe in a future reality in the present moment. You have to really feel the emotions of your future. This is not an intellectual process—it is a visceral one. What do you believe you're worthy to receive? Can you teach your body emotionally what it will feel like to receive what it is you want before it happens? In order for it to manifest, you have to be able to do this in the present moment.[55]

When we live our lives in gratitude, we are praising and thanking God continuously, as we were instructed to do. I'm not sure about manifesting the future, but I have expressed gratitude for what's to come and can attest to the blessings poured out on me since I found gratitude. Why would it be a surprise that our blessings would multiply if we follow Paul's sound advice?

"May the God of hope fill you with all joy and peace as you trust in him, so that you may overflow with hope by the power of the Holy Spirit."

ROMANS 15:13 NIV

Gratitude is such an amazing gift from God that when we realize and express it, we are blessed with even more. All too

---

55   Dr. Joe Dispenza (@DrJoeDispenzaOfficialNewsFanPage). August 2, 2019. "Gratitude is a Powerful Emotion to Use...."

often, people get in their heads that abundance has to do with wealth and prosperity, but when we look at the abundance gratitude can bring, it goes far beyond anything that can be bought, traveled to, or earned. Furthermore, God's will for us is to live life in his abundant love and therefore be a beacon to others.

"As the Father has loved me, so have I loved you. Abide in my love."

JOHN 15:9 ESV

We can either be bitter and judgmental or grateful—praising God for all his blessings. Gratitude tends to take people beyond themselves. Many who practice gratitude develop a need to help others. Being a blessing to others is how we ourselves are blessed. The Bible is clear about what will come of the path we choose:

"Give, and it will be given to you. A good measure, pressed down, shaken together and running over, will be poured into your lap. For with the measure you use, it will be measured to you."

LUKE 6:38 NIV

The abundance that Tolle and Dispenza describe has not been extensively studied. However, I can speak for myself and many others I have spoken to and interviewed in this book— when you practice gratitude in a meaningful way, unexpected blessings will appear in your life. It's a snowball effect, so to speak. And when you pray for and have gratitude for things that have not yet happened, all while trusting God's path, get ready to be amazed at the outcome. Please don't confuse this with the prosperity gospel teachings that some preach, because God promises *spiritual* blessings rather than *material* blessings, but know Jesus himself said:

"I have come that they may have life and have it to the full."

The next chapter will discuss the how-tos of this exact scenario.

CHAPTER 9

IMPLEMENTATION

"Whenever you can't think of something to be grateful for, remember your breath. With each breath you take, you can say, 'I'm still here.' Make each day a holiday of thankfulness—and give yourself the gift of gratitude!"

—OPRAH WINFREY

BOOMERANG

The implementation of gratitude is exemplified by David Meltzer's extraordinary story. Interestingly, gratitude was a cornerstone in his life as a child, but as an adult, he temporarily lost sight of it. Growing up without much, he knew he wanted to be wealthy to help his mom, so he worked hard and went to law school. Once out of school, he had a chance to join a startup in the internet and law space, and although his mother meant well when trying to deter him, stating the "internet will be a fad," he took that job and set himself on a quick upward trajectory.

Meltzer had amassed a large fortune as a successful attorney and businessman. He was later known as the CEO of the first smartphone company, and the world was his oyster. Like many others enjoying success at the time, he invested in golf courses and real estate, leveraging his wealth to invest in more. But when the real estate bubble burst, he lost everything—filing for bankruptcy soon after. After overhearing a conversation between his wife and her uncle about whether or not he could succeed with his back against the wall, he was reminded that he could rebuild and get back to a place of financial security. But he first needed to set a plan in place.

Taking stock of his life at this time, Meltzer recalled how happy his childhood was. He was raised as one of six kids by a single mother who constantly encouraged her kids to look at the glass as half full instead of half empty. As kids, they would come downstairs in the morning, and if any of them had a negative attitude, their mom would send them back to their room to come down and try it again. They were taught to say thank you and be grateful for everything.

What an important point. Far too often we say thank you as a conditioned response, but how often do we feel what we are saying?

Remembering his foundation of gratitude as a child is how gratitude became a pillar of Meltzer's success principles.

His goal became to treat gratitude as a muscle. But, at first, he forced it. Many people commit to something they don't feel like doing but know it's good for them, like going to the gym. They force themselves to get off the couch, not knowing how they will summon the energy or mental state to spend time there. They get through it, however, and feel better little by little. At some point, things shift, and they no longer see it as a task but as a habit. Others even get to a point where they look forward to participating in this habit.

I can relate to Meltzer's analogy. When I started to run, I didn't enjoy it at all. It was truly forced, but I scheduled time—even ten minutes here and there throughout my day—and running indoors prevented the excuse of bad weather. I even watched TV shows I was looking forward to catching up on as motivation to get through the drudgery. This distraction technique worked. Before I knew it, I *had* to get a run in at times, especially if I needed a mental break or had overindulged. It turned from a chore into a need. Nine years later, I run two and a half hours every week.

I'm still waiting to look forward to it, but I do notice the difference in my energy levels if I skip even a few days.

When first reimplementing gratitude into his life, Meltzer would catch himself turning negative and have to stop and say, "I'm so blessed," "I get to do this," and "I have this experience and these people in my life to help me learn and grow." Gratitude grew more natural, and the glass became half full again the majority of times. That's not to say everyone doesn't have bad days, but after consistent practice, Meltzer found it easy to shift back into the grateful mind-set when things would take a negative turn.

"Now I'm an ultramarathon runner of gratitude," he proclaims. "I went from a completely scarce and ego-based consciousness to someone who lives a centered existence and is constantly in a mind-set of abundance."

He gave me a quick glimpse of his upcoming week for his book launch—a segment on *The World's Greatest Motivators* with Les Brown and Bob Proctor, interviews with the New York Stock Exchange, and talks with Danica Patrick and Gary Vaynerchuk. With a contented sigh, he continued, "My life is a miracle."

I could feel the gratitude as he spoke with me; he was tapped in and living it, not losing sight of how blessed he was even in chaos.

Meltzer has gone from losing $100 million to cofounding Sports 1 Marketing with pro football Hall of Fame quarterback Warren Moon. Most importantly, gratitude is his number one core philosophy. The catalyst of gratitude boosted him up and beyond his prior success. When I asked about his goals and ambitions going forward, he answered, "My main inspiration is gratitude-based happiness, and my mission in life is to truly impact one thousand people to not only be happy through gratitude but to empower another one thousand people with the tools to obtain happiness, peace, and joy through gratitude, empathy, accountability, and effective communication."

Meltzer has done the mathematical calculations and wholeheartedly believes he can change the world through teaching and empowering others. His motivational hook is a simple one: "What if I could guarantee you happiness from the moment you wake up until you go to bed? Would it be enough?"

Acknowledgment from the majority of the audience is always the reaction to his hook, as most people at their core just want to be happy. He goes on to present his formula. Gratitude is the first and most important pillar because "it gives you perspective, and you realize everything doesn't always happen as expected." Second is empathy and forgiveness, which starts with forgiving yourself, as you can't give what you don't have for yourself. He learned early on that he needed to ease up and not expect of others what he expected of himself. One needs to empower others to have balance. Third is accountability, and he suggests asking yourself, "What did I do to attract this into my life, and what do I need to learn from it?"

The last pillar is effective communication, which is "an ability to connect with others as well as with whatever inspires you."

These four pillars are a critical part of his company, and every intern who comes on is taught this first and foremost. The program hinges on values, culture, and a mission to encourage people "to empower others to be happy."

Meltzer is a true guru of gratitude, so my final question to him was: if you are in the lowest of low places and you want to start, how do you do it? His advice is to focus on your breath. Starting there, he explains, you can stop all the noise and just be grateful for life itself. It can be the start of a small but powerful reminder that without breath, nothing else is possible. We are alive, and that in and of itself is a miracle.

Meltzer emphasizes that everyone should start and end their day with gratitude in any way possible, but we can begin and recap by focusing on what we have and set ourselves up for a positive, grateful mind-set that can be strengthened daily until it becomes an effective muscle.

The wisdom I take from Meltzer's story and experience is a reminder that we can start anywhere, and he, like so many others, found gratitude at the lowest points in his life. His story is also a reminder that gratitude must be felt to be most effective, and when you truly feel gratitude, your life starts to change in a positive way.

My mission is similar, and I too hope to share with as many people as possible the lasting positive effects that gratitude can have on one's life.

WHERE TO BEGIN

START WITH YOUR BREATH—WEEK ONE

Where to begin your gratitude journey? A great place to start is with your breath. No matter what is going on in your life, you can be grateful for your breath, your heartbeat, and go from there. If nothing else, you have something to build on. Oprah suggests this as the starting point to cultivating gratitude as well. And as we just found out, like working out, we need to start somewhere and build on it to grow the gratitude "muscle." I started this way, and to this day, I begin my gratitude practice by breathing.

Your breath is not only something to be grateful for but focusing on breathing also brings you out of fight-or-flight and into the present moment. Therefore it's a cornerstone in meditation practices. When you have a focal point that can take you away from all the thoughts going on in your head—the to-do lists, the noise—you begin to shut out all the distractions.

As you breathe in and out, you can feel the air filling and leaving your lungs. Count to five as you slowly inhale, then hold for five, then exhale slowly. I suggest you count to seven on the exhale. This will ensure you are using your full lung capacity, and over time, you will feel yourself moving from the sympathetic state (fight-or-flight) to the parasympathetic state (rest and digest). You should feel your heart rate slowing if you were in an anxious place.

When you feel yourself relax, you can begin thinking of all the processes taking place in your body that you are normally unaware of. Your lungs bring oxygen to your heart, which in turn pumps it to all the cells of your body. As your cells exchange it for carbon dioxide, it is then taken back to the lungs and exhaled. The simplest of processes is a place to feel gratitude. Think of all that happens to keep us alive that we never even give thought to! No matter what is going on in our lives, we can feel grateful for this.

When you first wake and before you go to bed are the times your subconscious and conscious mind are both accessible. You can do this for five to ten minutes each morning and evening for the first week.

NEXT, LET IT GO—WEEK TWO

You will still begin with the breathing, although you may not need as much time to get into the relaxed state the more you practice. Once relaxed, you are ready to add the next phase.

Anxieties, worries, negative thoughts, anything you are thinking that isn't serving you must be relinquished. When we free up this space from an energy perspective, we create room for positive emotions, including gratitude.

"We demolish arguments and every pretension that sets itself up against the knowledge of God, and we take captive every thought to make it obedient to Christ."

2 CORINTHIANS 10:5 NIV

During your morning and evening routine, make a conscious effort to think of the negative things that are stuck in your head. Don't let yourself go to that mind-set but become aware

and curious about those things. Then visualize them disconnecting from you like a balloon on a string, floating away
until you let go of the string and watch that negative thought
disappear. I also like the analogy of dropping a leaf into a
stream and watching it float away. Each negative thought or
feeling should be held and then consciously released as we
ask God to take it, giving thanks as he does.

*"Do not be anxious about anything, but in every situation, by
prayer and petition, with thanksgiving, present your requests to
God. And the peace of God, which transcends all understanding, will guard your hearts and your minds in Christ Jesus."*
PHILIPPIANS 4:6–7 NIV

Thank God for the release of these thoughts to make room for
the positive. Relish in the peace brought by the release of that
thought and praise God for it being gone. Go through this
exercise multiple times if some of the deep-rooted negative
thoughts still stick. If possible in this time, choose to forgive.
As stated in the beginning of the book, if you have been hurt
deeply, you may need to go through a deeper forgiveness routine first. When we can forgive everyone who has wronged
us as well as ourselves, we can be truly free.

Once you have gone through each negative thought that you
can remember, take that gratitude and move to the next level.

GUIDED GRATITUDE PRACTICE—WEEK THREE AND ONWARD

Give yourself ten to fifteen minutes initially, working up to
thirty to forty-five minutes eventually. This is not a require-
ment every day, but during the first four to six weeks, you will

want to get to thirty or forty-five minutes ideally, building the gratitude muscle. The better you get, the less time you will need, and if you are going through a crisis or rough time, you may need to dedicate more time to this exercise.

First, find a comfortable, quiet place, free of distractions. I also suggest that you be sitting, as I have heard from many that you may fall asleep if you try this step lying down. You want to remain awake, although this can help you wind down prior to bed.

Keep a log each day with this phase for the first few weeks. Notice how you are feeling, your energy, contentment, and sleep quality and jot down notes. Break it down into each section we covered in this book and rate each one on a scale of one to ten. Circle one option each day. See the notes section below to add any additional things you may notice:

Self-Worth:	1	2	3	4	5	6	7	8	9	10
Mental Health:	1	2	3	4	5	6	7	8	9	10
Physical Health:	1	2	3	4	5	6	7	8	9	10
Ability to Handle Adversity:	1	2	3	4	5	6	7	8	9	10
Connection to Others:	1	2	3	4	5	6	7	8	9	10
Happiness:	1	2	3	4	5	6	7	8	9	10
Abundance:	1	2	3	4	5	6	7	8	9	10

Notes:

_____

_____

_____

_____

_____

Continue to repeat the breathing exercise and the release of any negative thoughts as the first two steps. You will get to the point that this doesn't take much time, unless you are going through a particularly tough situation at the time and need to spend more time releasing the negative.

Additionally, at this stage, if you want to learn a new task in unison with your gratitude practice, it may prove beneficial, as learning is etched into the brain in much the same way. Have you ever wanted to learn how to play an instrument, juggle, or adopt another new skill? Now is a great time!

* * *

Think of a memory that is so good you can feel it—if you concentrate, you may feel warm or get goosebumps. For me, I recall a moment on vacation with my kids when we were all on a float together at a water park, laughing and close. I can smell the sunscreen if I close my eyes. Vividly, I feel the warmth of my kids' skin against mine. Happiness floods into my body.

Recall every detail you can from that moment. What were you wearing? What was the weather like? Who was with you, and what are the details of their clothes, hair, and actions? Fill in the details based on what you remember. What did you see, hear, feel, smell, or taste? Going through each sense is a great way to immerse yourself in the memory.

Take this memory in with every part of your being, giving thanks to God for all the blessings you are reexperiencing. It takes practice, but the more details you can recall, the more this memory will impact you in the present.

Now take that feeling and project it into the future. What are you praying and hoping for? Let your mind go there with this feeling. Give thanks to God for the events that are yet to happen. Don't go into detail, as God is in control. Let him surprise you. Again, relish that feeling in full thanksgiving to God. Try to stay in this place for as long as you can. Hold the feeling. As you are experiencing this, be aware of how you feel and stay in a place of gratitude.

Use different starting memories each time, so, if necessary, take time to reflect on the memories you will be using. This exercise marries the practice of gratitude with neuroplasticity, and it has been the most impactful and useful practice by far for my health and well-being. The more you do this, the longer you can keep that feeling going.

GRATITUDE AND NEUROPLASTICITY 2.0

By focusing on a positive memory and coupling it with a hope for the future, we can create our own reality of happiness, joy, and fulfillment. Gratitude is a key component.

THE POWER OF SMELL

Smell is perceived as the least-needed sense, yet many argue that it's the strongest. No other sense ties directly into the limbic system and memory like the sense of smell does. Without smell, we cannot taste food beyond salty, sweet, and bitter—there is no other dimension.

Most people think losing their sense of sight would be much more devastating, and initially it is, however, over time, those who lose their sense of smell are much more depressed than those who lose their sight according to Dr. Rachel Herz, a cognitive neuroscientist and psychologist. She has studied smell for decades and written several books, including *The Scent of Desire* and *Why You Eat What You Eat.*

"Smell is the only sense hardwired to your emotional center and directly connects to the amygdala," Herz says. Smells can evoke the most emotional memories. We have all had that experience where we catch a whiff of a certain scent and it immediately takes us to a vivid, detailed memory. One of those for me is the scent of chlorine in an indoor pool. Every time I smell it, it takes me back to the days I swam competitively, and it's so invigorating, I immediately feel a surge of energy and excitement.

Interestingly enough for Dr. Herz, the scent of a skunk brings back fond childhood memories for her. As a young girl, just prior to smelling a skunk odor for the first time, her mother exclaimed, "I love that smell," and ever since, that has been etched in her emotional center as a pleasant memory. She also knew she would marry her husband when she first smelled him, and research indicates that we are attracted to mates through our sense of smell.[56]

Conversely, smells can be one of the worst triggers for PTSD. Some soldiers who have been in war cannot tolerate barbeques because it takes them back to a traumatic time during

---

56 Skimbaco. "Scents of Fall—Interview with Rachel Herz, Expert on the on the Psychology of Smell."

the war. Losing your sense of smell can also be the first symptom of Alzheimer's and Parkinson's. Herz cites a study where people over fifty-seven who had a poor sense of smell were four times more likely to die within a five-year period than those with a good sense of smell.[57]

Herz suggests we can create a pallet of pleasant scent "memories," but we need to rotate them, so they don't lose their effectiveness. I believe we can pair scents that evoke a strong emotion with gratitude to pull ourselves more strongly and quickly into happiness.

This can complement the practice you learned in week three. You may want to proactively think of a few smells that take you to a happy memory and put them in the notes section. Is the smell of suntan lotion, baby powder, or pumpkin spice associated with a happy memory? Let the details of a memory come rushing back with the smell.

FEEL THE EMOTIONS, FOCUS ON ALL THE SENSES

Beyond smell, all the senses can be powerful in recalling our most treasured memories. The rewiring happens much quicker and is more effective when these tactics are implemented.

In his book *Hardwiring Happiness*, Dr. Rick Hanson suggests relishing happy "passing experiences" as jewels and participating in the mental exercise of taking each memory and putting it in a box next to our hearts. He suggests staying in

---

57   Dara R. Adams, et al. "Olfactory Dysfunction Predicts Subsequent Dementia in Older US adults." (140)

this moment for at least twelve seconds rather than letting it pass by. Hanson states that the brain has a "negativity bias," which means that it's inherently easier to take in a negative experience and learn from it than it is to take in a positive one and learn, so we need to consciously do the latter. The more Hanson would note and take in these positive experiences, feeling the positive emotion, the more they would affect his happiness for the better.

He created the acronym HEAL, which means: *Have* a good experience, *enrich* it (let it grow for several seconds), *absorb* it (feel it), *link* it (with another experience). This boils down to what Hanson says is simply, "Have it, enjoy it." Doing this will prime your memory systems to improve their neural structure.[58]

GRATITUDE TO COMBAT STRESS OR ANXIETY (QUICK FIX)

TEN SECONDS

Counting to ten while reflecting on something you are grateful for is incredibly effective. Five seconds is about the time it takes to identify the negative situation, and another five is needed to replace it with something you are thankful for. One easy thing to do is keep a photo that invokes gratitude as your phone's screen saver so that it's easily accessible when needed. This short but quick antidote to stress and anxiety can also help build your gratitude muscle over time.

---

58 TEDx Talks "Hardwiring Happiness: Dr. Rick Hanson at *TEDxMarin* 2013."

WRITE THREE NOTES

If you have more time, you can take a few minutes to write three thank-you notes to people who deserve them in your life. Just the exercise of writing them will take you out of the negative mind-set, but if you take the extra step to also deliver them, you will be amazed by what comes back to you.

NATURE

The natural world evokes awe. The plants, animals, weather patterns, and seasons are all miracles to observe. A short five- to ten-minute walk is incredibly therapeutic when you are viewing things through the lens of gratitude. If you aren't able to get outside, you can sit by a window and practice the same exercise—although it's not as effective.

NEXT LEVEL

DON'T KEEP IT TO YOURSELF

The transformation that gratitude brought to my life has caused me to want to be of service to as many others as I can. Gratitude multiplies as you share it. We learned that the expression of gratitude connects us to others in Chapter 6. When you are going through your day, take time to show gratitude for everything and to everyone you can. You will find it's often appreciated and reciprocated, and this will quickly become a habit.

WE HAVE BEEN INSTRUCTED ALREADY

The Bible instructs us in Luke 10:27 that love is the key—to love God with all our hearts and our neighbor as ourselves.

But it also states in 1 Thessalonians that we should praise God continuously, give thanks to him in every circumstance, and be humble—giving all credit to God. This is where we are instructed to bring gratitude into our lives. As I have discovered and I hope you will too, gratitude, God's gift, has brought more happiness to my life than I ever thought possible.

I pray that this chapter will guide you as you implement gratitude as a pillar in your life. Although it's broken down into three weeks for learning purposes, please remember that the practice of gratitude needs to happen daily to maintain its positive effect in your life.

CHAPTER 10

TYING IT ALL TOGETHER

"You are responsible for your own happiness."

—UNKNOWN

ENOUGH

Gratitude is so powerful, it can turn "just enough" not only into sufficient but also into a wealth of happiness and contentment. Case in point is Warren Buffett, who is, as of June 18, 2019, the third wealthiest person in the world with a staggering net worth of $82 billion. Yet he lives in the same Omaha house he purchased for $31.5K in 1958 and gets a childish grin on his face telling people it's the third-best investment he ever made. "I'm happy here. If I thought I could be happier somewhere else, I would move," Buffett says.

He drives an average Cadillac XTS with a retail price of $45K and is involved in many philanthropic endeavors, primarily the Bill & Melinda Gates Foundation. He founded the giving pledge in 2009 with Bill Gates, where billionaires pledge to give away at least half of their earnings. He has personally taken this pledge to the extreme and vowed to give away over ninety-nine percent of all he has amassed.

"If you're in the luckiest one percent of humanity, you owe it to the rest of humanity to think about the other ninety-nine percent."

—WARREN BUFFETT

To this day, he is still known for his frugality. According to CNBC, he never pays more than $3.17 for breakfast, thanks to McDonald's.[59] Buffett credits gratitude and sharing his success to his long-lasting fortune. We can learn a lot from someone who has been so successful but hasn't fallen into the trap of worldly possessions and the "more is better" mentality. Buffett's story is truly inspirational for me. With enough, you can be content, happy, and make the world a better place for others with your excess.

REMEMBER

"Gratitude is so central to the life that God has made for us. Until we can center ourselves on what we do have, on what God has given us, on the life we do get to live, we'll constantly be looking for another life. That is why the word 'remember' occurs again and again in the Bible. God commands his people to remember who they are, where they've been, what they've seen, and what's been done for them. If we stop remembering, we may forget. And that's when the trouble comes."

—ROB BELL

Through this journey of gratitude, I have been blessed to connect with many others who have had a similar pilgrimage. The one constant I've observed in every single person is the spiritual awakening they have all experienced through finding gratitude and an amazing connection to God.

In life, we lose loved ones, life zigs when we expect a zag, and bad things happen. How we react to these things can mold

---

59   Kathleen Elkins. "Warren Buffett Eats the Same Thing for Breakfast Every Day—and It Never Costs More than $3.17."

and shape us. We can emerge a stronger person or shrivel and retract into our shells.

Matt was fourteen when he lost his baby sister at only seven months of age. Over the next several years, he would lose a young family friend who was like an uncle to him, his grandfather, and finally his mother when she was fifty-four.

Funerals had become commonplace, but his mother's funeral hit Matt hard. Over a thousand people showed up, and they all came up to the family to express how his mom had impacted their lives. She had been an integral part of the church and volunteered often, especially in the children's ministry. People kept coming to share their stories, appreciation, and condolences. The family received emails and texts after the funeral for weeks from others saying they waited hours to talk to them, had to leave for work, but still wanted to share.

"That is where everything changed for me. I was like, wait a minute, I am not having the right appreciation for the things in my life," Matt said.

Finding gratitude in that moment was life-altering for Matt. "It propelled me forward with gratitude for all I had. God is real, and we choose how we react to our circumstances." He describes God shifting his perspective, and he knew he was being called into ministry. Gratitude began to sink in even further for him.

The more he studied Scripture, the more grateful he became, knowing the ultimate price Christ paid for our sins and living in the hope of grace and eternity to come. "Such a great grace has been given to me. How can I hold back sharing it with others?" He looked back and saw how judgmental and close-minded he had been. Matt equates the gospel with attending funerals—many have been to funerals of people they knew, but until you have attended one from someone so impactful in your life, like your own mother, you don't really get it. Going through the motions so to speak. Such is the gospel.

Although many of us read the Bible and were raised with it, until you really let the words sink in and understand what we have been given, we don't really get it. We need to turn off autopilot. And through that perspective and profound gratitude, we can fully live.

What strikes me most about Matt's story is the impact that gratitude had on him at such a young age. Perspective is everything. Our lens can either portray negative or positive, and the choice is always ours. This is why I'm so passionate about teaching gratitude to kids.

In this book, we have explored how gratitude can change your self-worth through Sam's story of addiction and rising from his lowest point to reach out and help others stuck in similar circumstances. We also heard Brené Brown's story in Chapter 2, and how vulnerability and gratitude changed her life.

In Chapter 3, we dove into a lot of science on our thought patterns and mental health. We learned how fear can be passed down genetically, the downside of social media, the effects of FOMO, and how positive and negative thoughts transform ice crystals. Tony Robbins's story showcased how we can use the power of gratitude to counteract fear, anxiety, and depression.

The mind/body connection came further into play in Chapter 4, where we learned the incredible healing journey of Joe Dispenza and how gratitude, in his opinion, is the strongest emotion we have to use. Dr. Bruce Lipton explained how gratitude can positively affect us at a cellular level in the aging process. We heard Nikki's story of mind-set over genetics through gratitude.

Adversity was discussed in Chapter 5, and we heard how Sheryl Sandberg and Matthew Maher both relied on gratitude to overcome unthinkable circumstances. Both came out on top and have used their stories as a tool to help others in profound ways.

We studied our connection to others in Chapter 6, and we heard the stories of Oprah, Kelly, and Andrew. Each found the gift of gratitude and the connection to others it brings forth. In all three cases, these incredible individuals have gone on to form a career around gratitude and connecting others.

Chapter 7 brought us to true happiness, and we heard the Dalai Lama's and Monique's stories. Two completely different lives rooted in gratitude, both profoundly showcasing how happy one can be regardless of former circumstances.

Abundance was the focus of Chapter 8, and the stories of Eckhart Tolle and Krista Woods were highlighted. Oprah also came back in, and Dr. Joe Dispenza broke down how gratitude ties into abundance. We found compelling evidence that gratitude, practiced in a meaningful way, can bring more blessings than any of us could imagine.

Finally, in Chapter 9, we learned how best to implement the practice of gratitude in our lives. We can't expect things to change overnight, but my hope is that you will make time to practice gratitude each day.

Gratitude is such an amazing gift from God, and we need to make room for it in the daily chaos to see the wonders it can bring forth. By reading this book, you have completed the first step of implementing gratitude into your life. If you haven't started yet, you are now equipped with the knowledge to do so. I pray that through the practice of gratitude you will see your life transformed as I have, and that you will flourish.

APPENDIX

INTRODUCTION

Allen, Mike. "Sean Parker Unloads on Facebook: 'God Only Knows What It's Doing to Our Children's Brains.'" *Axios*. Published November 9, 2017. *www.axios.com/ sean-parker-unloads-on-facebook-god-only-knows-what- its-doing-to-our-childrens-brains-1513306792-f855e7b4-4e99- 4d60-8d51-2775559c2671.html.*

Centers for Disease Control and Prevention. "Suicide Mortality in the United States 1999-2017 Centers for Disease Control and Prevention. Published October 3, 2018. *www.cdc.gov/ nchs/products/databriefs/db330.htm.*

GETTING THE MOST OUT OF THIS BOOK

"The Hawaiian Secret of Forgiveness." *Psychology Today*. Sussex Publishers. Accessed December 19, 2019. *https://www. psychologytoday.com/us/blog/focus-forgiveness/201105/the- hawaiian-secret-forgiveness.*

CHAPTER 1

Barton, Lynn M., Joan E. Sassone and Mary Hasek Grenier. "Gratitude." *Images of America Webster.* Arcadia Publishing, 2010.

Barton, Lynn M., Joan E. Sassone and Mary Hasek Grenier. "Neuroplasticity." *Images of America Webster.* Arcadia Publishing, 2010.

Brickman, Philip, et al. "Lottery Winners and Accident Victims: Is Happiness Relative?" *Journal of Personality and Social Psychology* 36, no. 8 (1978): 917–927. *https://doi. org/10.1037//0022-3514.36.8.917*

Clarke, Carrie D. "How Gratitude Actually Changes Your Brain and Is Good for Business." Thrive Global. Published February 7, 2018. *www.thriveglobal.com/stories/how-gratitude-actually-changes-your-brain-and-is-good-for-business*

Emmons, Robert, Robert Emmons, University of California, and University of California. "Why Gratitude Is Good." Greater Good. Accessed October 22, 2019. *https://greatergood. berkeley.edu/article/item/why_gratitude_is_good*

TodaSyo, "Matthieu Ricard's Approach to Meditation (Mystical Brain)" *YouTube Video,* Accessed July 19, 2019. *https://www. youtube.com/watch?v=5xifMxRz-_g*

CHAPTER 2

Brown, Brené. "Dr. Brené Brown "Joy: It's Terrifying." *SuperSoulSunday.* Oprah.com. Accessed January 4, 2020. *http://www.oprah.com/own-super-soul-sunday/dr-brene-brown-on-joy-its-terrifying-video*

Brown, Brené. "Brené Brown on Joy and Gratitude." Global Leadership Network, November 19, 2018. Accessed on

January 3, 2020. *https://globalleadership.org/articles/leading-yourself/brene-brown-on-joy-and-gratitude/*

Brown, Brené. "Dr. Brené Brown: 'Shame Is Lethal.'" *SuperSoulSunday.* Oprah.com. Accessed January 2, 2020. *http://www.oprah.com/own-super-soul-sunday/dr-brene-brown-shame-is-lethal-video.*

Brown, Brené. "The Power of Vulnerability." TED. Accessed September 5, 2019. *http://www.ted.com/talks/brene_brown_the_power_of_vulnerability?language=en*

Heinz, Adrienne J., Elizabeth R. Disney, David H. Epstein, Louise A. Glezen, Pamela I. Clark, and Kenzie L. Preston. "A Focus-Group Study on Spirituality and Substance-User Treatment." *Substance Use & Misuse* 45, no. 1-2 (2010): 134-153. *https://dx.doi.org/10.3109%2F10826080903035130*

.Roosevelt, Theodore "Theodore Roosevelt's The Man in the Arena Speech: 100th Anniversary," Leading Blog, published April 23, 2010, accessed February 5, 2020.

CHAPTER 3

Allen, Mike. "Sean Parker Unloads on Facebook: 'God Only Knows What It's Doing to Our Children's Brains.'" *Axios.* Published November 9, 2017. *www.axios.com/sean-parker-unloads-on-facebook-god-only-knows-what-its-doing-to-our-childrens-brains-1513306792-f855e7b4-4e99-4d60-8d51-2775559c2671.html*Damania, Zubin. "Are Zombie Doctors Taking over America?" *TEDMED.* Accessed August 27, 2019. *https://www.tedmed.com/talks/show?id=34752*

Dias, Brian G., and Kerry J. Ressler. "Parental Olfactory Experience Influences Behavior and Neural Structure in Subsequent Generations." *Nature Neuroscience* 17, no. 1 (2014):89–96. *https://www.ncbi.nlm.nih.gov/pmc/articles/PMC3923835/.*

Emoto, Masaru. *The Hidden Messages in Water*. Simon and Schuster, 2011.

Feloni, Richard. "Tony Robbins Gives Every Entrepreneur the Same Two Pieces of Advice." *Business Insider*. Business Insider, September 29, 2017. *https://www.businessinsider.com/tony-robbins-advice-to-entrepreneurs-2017-9*.

Feloni, Richard. "Tony Robbins Started out as a Broke Janitor—Then He Saved a Week's Worth of Pay, and the Way He Spent It Changed His Life." *Business Insider*. Business Insider, October 4, 2017. *https://www.businessinsider.com/tony-robbins-changed-his-life-at-17-years-old-2017-10*

Green, Sarah. "Epigenetics." In Google. Bellwether Media, Inc., 2016.

Huddleston, Tom Jr. "This Is Tony Robbins's 10-Minute Morning Routine to 'Change Your Day for the Better.'" *CNBC*. Accessed April 9, 2019. *https://www.cnbc.com/2019/04/09/tony-robbins-10-minute-morning-routine-to-get-in-a-peak-state.html*.

Lewis, Robert. "Tony Robbins." *Encyclopædia Britannica*. Encyclopædia Britannica, Inc., July 16, 2019. *https://www.britannica.com/biography/Tony-Robbins*.

Radin, Dean, Gail Hayssen, Masaru Emoto, and Takashige Kizu. "Double-Blind Test of the Effects of Distant Intention on Water Crystal Formation." *Explore 2*, no. 5 (2006): 408-411. *https://doi.org/10.1016/j.explore.2006.06.004*.

Robbins, Tony. *The Mentors Who Coached Me*. tonyrobbins.com, October 2, 2019. *https://www.tonyrobbins.com/mind-meaning/the-mentors-who-coached-me/*

Yehuda, Rachel, et. al. "Transgenerational Effects of Posttraumatic Stress Disorder in Babies of Mothers Exposed to the World Trade Center Attacks during Pregnancy." *The*

Journal of Clinical Endocrinology & Metabolism 90, no. 7 (2005): 4115–4118. *https://doi.org/10.1210/jc.2005-0550*

ZdoggMD. "What Is Social Media Doing to Our Daughters?" YouTube video. Accessed July 7, 2019. *https://www.youtube. com/watch?v=dlI6vI7gSRM*

CHAPTER 4

American Physiological Society (APS). "Mind over Matter: Can You Think Your Way to Strength?" *Science Daily*. Published December 31, 2014. Accessed January 27, 2020. *https://www. sciencedaily.com/releases/2014/12/141231154012.htm*.

Dispenza, Joe. *The Power of Gratitude*. Dr. Joe Dispenza's Blog, February 6, 2017. Accessed July 6, 2019. *https://drjoedispenza. net/blog/health/the-power-of-gratitude*.

Dispenza, Joe. "How I Healed Myself After Breaking 6 Vertebrae: The Placebo Effect in Action." *You Can Heal Your Life*. Accessed August 9, 2019. *https://www.healyourlife.com/ how-i-healed-myself-after-breaking-6-vertebrae*.

Emmons, Robert A, McCullough, Michael E. "Counting Blessings vs. Burdens: An Experimental Investigation of Gratitude and Subjective Well-Being in Daily Life." *Journal of Personality and Social Psychology* 2003, Vol 84, No. 2, 377-389. *https://greatergood.berkeley.edu/images/application_ uploads/Emmons-CountingBlessings.pdf*

Hill, Patrick L., Mathias Allemand, and Brent W. Roberts. "Examining the Pathways Between Gratitude and Self-Rated Physical Health Across Adulthood." *Personality and Individual Differences* 54, no. 1 (2013): 92-96. *https://doi. org/10.1016/j.paid.2012.08.011*.

Leaf, Caroline. *Switch on Your Brain: The Key to Peak Happiness, Thinking, and Health*. Baker Books, 2013.

Lipton, Bruce H. "The Healing Power of Gratitude—Bruce Lipton Explains Telomeres", YouTube Video, Accessed September 1, 2019. *https://www.youtube.com/watch?v=vEfXK3D8vGc.*

Real, London "DR JOE DISPENZA—HOW I HEALED MYSELF | London Real," *YouTube Video*, Accessed August 9, 2019. *https://www.youtube.com/watch?v=-WVu-OzCE9Y.*

"The Effects of Stress on Your Body." WebMD. Accessed December 10, 2019. *https://www.webmd.com/balance/stress-management/effects-of-stress-on-your-body.*

CHAPTER 5

Aitkenhead, Decca. 2017. "Sheryl Sandberg: 'Everyone Looked at Me like I Was a Ghost.'" *The Guardian.* Guardian News and Media. April 16, 2017. https://www.theguardian.com/technology/2017/apr/16/sheryl-sandberg-facebook-everyone-looked-at-me-like-a-ghost.

Beheshti, Naz. "Science Says You Shouldn't Wait for Things to Go Well Before Showing Gratitude." *Forbes,* November 25, 2019. Accessed December 15, 2019. *https://www.forbes.com/sites/nazbeheshti/2019/11/25/science-says-you-shouldnt-wait-for-things-to-go-well-before-showing-gratitude/#6435095c3c5b*

Brooks, Arthur C. "Choose to Be Grateful. It Will Make You Happier." *New York Times.* Published November 21, 2015. *https://www.nytimes.com/2015/11/22/opinion/sunday/choose-to-be-grateful-it-will-make-you-happier.html*

O'Dea, Meghan. "Transcript: Sheryl Sandberg at the University of California at Berkeley 2016 Commencement." *Fortune.* Fortune, May 19, 2016. *https://fortune.com/2016/05/14/sandberg-uc-berkley-transcript/*

Shapiro, Ari. "'Just Show Up': Sheryl Sandberg On How To Help Someone Who's Grieving." *NPR.* NPR, April 25, 2017.

*https://www.npr.org/2017/04/25/525453115/just-show-up-sheryl-
sandberg-on-how-to-help-someone-whos-grieving*

CHAPTER 6

Brower, Tracy. "Yes, Social Media Is Making You Miserable."
Fast Company, October 28, 2019. *https://www.fastcompany.
com/90415438/yes-social-media-is-making-you-miserable*

Franchina, Vittoria, Mariek Vanden Abeele, Antonius J. Van
Rooij, Gianluca Lo Coco, and Lieven De Marez. "Fear of
Missing Out as a Predictor of Problematic Social Media
Use and Phubbing Behavior Among Flemish Adolescents."
*International Journal of Environmental Research and
Public Health* 15, no. 10 (2018): 2319. *https://doi.org/10.3390/
ijerph15102319*

Fry, Elizabeth. "Did Oprah's Childhood Shape Her Career?"
LiveAbout. LiveAbout, August 22, 2019. *https://www.
liveabout.com/childhood-biography-of-oprah-winfrey-2535832*

Holmes, Lindsay. "10 Things Grateful People Do Differently."
HuffPost. Updated November 28, 2018. *https://www.huffpost.
com/entry/habits-of-grateful-people_n_565352a6e4b0d4093a
588538*Van Wolkenten, Megan, Sarah F. Brosnan, and Frans
BM de Waal. "Inequity Responses of Monkeys Modified by
Effort." Proceedings of the National Academy of Sciences
104, no. 47 (2007): 18854-18859. *https://doi.org/10.1073/
pnas.0707182104*

CHAPTER 7

Harvard Health Publishing. "Giving Thanks Can Make You
Happier." Harvard Health. Accessed January 27, 2020.
*https://www.health.harvard.edu/healthbeat/giving-thanks-
can-make-you-happier.*

Health Resources & Services Administration. "The 'Loneliness Epidemic.'" January 17, 2019. *https://www.hrsa.gov/enews/ past-issues/2019/january-17/loneliness-epidemic.*

"Questions & Answers." The 14th Dalai Lama, Accessed July 18, 2019. *https://www.dalailama.org/the-dalai-lama/biography-and-daily-life/questions-answers.*

CHAPTER 8

Dispenza, Dr. Joe (@DrJoeDispenzaOfficialNewsFanPage). "Gratitude is a powerful emotion to use for manifesting because normally we feel gratitude...- Dr Joe Dispenza—OFFICIAL NEWS & FAN PAGE. Accessed June 28, 2019. *https://www.facebook.com/ DrJoeDispenzaOfficialNewsFanPage/posts/gratitude-is-a-powerful-emotion-to-use-for-manifesting-because-normally-we-feel-/3440111496014220/.*

Peacefulness "Eckhart Tolle and Oprah Winfrey—Abundance and Gratitude", YouTube Video, Accessed October 1, 2019. *https://www.youtube.com/watch?v=ihKFOgL5amI.*

Pickle, Clarified "Eckhart Tolle & His Enlightenment—How It Happened", YouTube Video, Accessed September 12, 2019. *https://www.youtube.com/watch?v=tSof9wAOTJs.*

CHAPTER 9

Adams, Dara R., David W. Kern, Kristen E. Wroblewski, Martha K. McClintock, William Dale, and Jayant M. Pinto. "Olfactory Dysfunction Predicts Subsequent Dementia in Older US Adults." *Journal of the American Geriatrics Society* 66, no. 1 (2018): 140-144. *https://dx.doi.org/10.1111%2Fjgs.15048.*

Skimbaco "Scents of Fall—Interview with Rachel Herz, Expert on the on the Psychology of Smell," YouTube Video, Accessed September 15, 2019. *https://www.youtube.com/ watch?v=kagoyF6hC8c.*

TEDx Talks "Hardwiring Happiness: Dr. Rick Hanson at
    TEDxMarin 2013" , YouTube Video, Accessed November 2,
    2019. *https://www.youtube.com/watch?v=jpuDyGgIeho.*

CHAPTER 10

Elkins, Kathleen. "Warren Buffett Eats the Same Thing for
    Breakfast Every Day—and It Never Costs More than
    $3.17." *CNBC.* CNBC, January 30, 2017. *https://www.cnbc.*
    com/2017/01/30/warren-buffetts-breakfast-never-costs-more-
    than-317.html

ADDITIONAL RESOURCES

Hardwiring Happiness Rick Hanson

The Brain that Changes Itself Norman Doidge

Switch on Your Brain Caroline Leaf

Breaking the Habit of Being Yourself Joe Dispenza

The Biology of Belief Bruce Lipton

Thanks! How the New Science of Gratitude Can Make You
    Happier Robert Emmons

The Hidden Messages in Water Masaru Emoto

Made in the USA
Columbia, SC
18 December 2020

28615544R00098